Elementary Horsemanship

Ford E. Young Jr.

FOREWORD

The youth of today and tomorrow will not have the advantages of the training in practical horsemanship which the Army has afforded to the author through the years, first as a student in the Cavalry Branch of the Citizens Military Training Camps during the Summers of 1924, 25 and 26; as a Reserve Cavalry Officer from 1933 to 1940; as a Cavalry Officer on active duty at Fort Riley, Kansas, from October of 1940 until September of 1943, including graduation from both the Basic and Advanced Horse Classes of the Cavalry School and riding as a member of the Cavalry School Hunt; and thereafter on the Staff of the 2nd Cavalry Division until being ordered overseas during January of 1944.

This book, therefore, is written for the purpose of passing on the lessons learned through these experiences in the same manner that the author has given instruction in elementary horsemanship to his relatives and friends since his return to inactive status as a reserve officer. The author's riding horses, which are referred to in this book, are his two faithful thoroughbred Army mounts "Reno Kit" and "Golden Tone", a big steady fourteen-year-old half-bred gelding named "Hercules" and an impetuous five-year-old granddaughter of "Man O War" named "Zola L".

FORD E. YOUNG, JR.

ELEMENTARY HORSEMANSHIP

TABLE OF CONTENTS

ELEMENTARY HORSEMANSHIP

Chapter I

INTRODUCTION

Before we concern ourselves with the features of riding by use of the balanced seat, it would be well for us to consider a few matters which are very important to the progress of a beginner as a horseman.

If you have any fear of riding horseback, it should be overcome. The principal fear of most inexperienced riders is the helpless feeling which results from having a horse run away with them. After we have considered the proper positions in the saddle and the correct way to hold your reins and use them at various gaits, I will explain to you the use of what we call the "emergency brake". Correct use of the reins will enable you to guide a horse, which has started to run away, in a circle. When you know how to guide a horse so that he is running in a circle and how to apply the emergency brake at the time when you desire to do so, there need be no fear of a horse running away with you.

Another fear of some inexperienced riders is that of falling from a horse. The answer to that is that the best of riders get a spill once in a while but that, unless you are trying to make a horse jump an obstacle beyond the state of his training, you can roll away from him as he falls or if you fall from him. It frequently does a timid rider a great deal of good to have one or two falls from a horse because it is unlikely that he will be hurt and, having learned that there is nothing to fear from a fall, he will become a more determined rider.

Let us now consider the unwillingness of some beginners to compel a horse to do what they want him to do. I have been surprised to see some young men who were otherwise good athletes but who could not squeeze a well trained and normally willing horse hard enough with their legs to cause him to go from a walk to a trot. The best answer to this is that the rider must be determined that he will compel the horse to obey him. This determination can be best exemplified by use of legs and voice and by coordination of the use of the rider's body and reins. It is valueless to squeeze a horse with your legs or kick him and shout "get up" while pulling back with the reins and leaning backwards with the body. I will tell you how to compel the horse to do what you want him to do as we consider the position of the rider, correct use of the reins and the other aids at the various gaits, and when we consider the matter of compelling horses to take jumps. For now, I wish to emphasize the fact that a beginner must be determined in his actions in order to make the best progress in practical horsemanship.

Another point for a beginner to bear in mind is the old theory that a horse thinks of only one thing at a time. Not long ago, I was holding the halter on my five-year-old thoroughbred "Zola L." while a blacksmith was shoeing her. She was well behaved until he had put on three shoes and had started to work on her right hind foot. Suddenly she put on a tirade which caused the blacksmith to lose hold of her foot and it took me several seconds to calm her down. Thereupon, I started talking to her and she became so much interested in listening that she behaved while he finished shoeing her. This is only one example of how a horse's mind can be occupied by one line of thought, thereby avoiding the necessity of drastic action. As long as you, as a rider, can keep your horse's mind on the quality of your ride at the desired gait you are likely to have pleasant riding. Correct use of your reins, correct posture in the saddle and correct use of the legs at each of the various gaits will enable you to keep the horse's mind on giving you the type of riding you desire.

Another theory to bear in mind is that a horse reacts, primarily, to two methods of treatment, namely, reward and punishment. This is particularly important in jumping, as we shall see when we discuss that subject, and it is unfortunate that much more can be accomplished by punishment than by reward in training a horse to jump. However, it is much better to take a few carrots or apples or a small amount of grain with you to get horses which are in pasture than to wear yourself out in an effort to reach them. When they see food, they will come to you and they should be rewarded by having you give it to them. Immediately after a horse has done what you wanted him to do he deserves a pat on the neck and a kind word. It is a particularly good practice to pat him and praise him when he has given you a pleasant trot or canter and when you come back down from either or both of these faster gaits to a walk. When dismounted you can, next to feeding your horse, best make friends with him by kind words and a rub around the back of his ears.

It is basic that, after a workout, a horse should be cooled off by being ridden at a walk or by being led. After he is cooled off, he should be given a drink of water and then be fed and groomed. This procedure, which is more fully explained in Chapter VIII, is the best reward for a horse and all too fre-

7

quently his natural gratitude goes to the stablehand who does the work and not to his owner or rider.

Chapter II

POSITION IN THE SADDLE

We will reserve to a subsequent chapter the explanation of adjusting equipment and the method of mounting and dismounting to be recommended so that we can get right into the most important part of this book. However, if you desire to study adjusting equipment, mounting and dismounting before becoming concerned with what to do when mounted, you may do so by turning to Chapter VII. The biggest mistakes made by most inexperienced or uninstructed riders are their failure to maintain a balanced seat while mounted and their failure to coordinate the maintaining of a balanced seat with the correct use of their reins.

Generally speaking by use of the words "balanced seat" we mean that the rider's weight is so placed that he is not out of balance to the front, the rear, or to the side, and that the position of his feet in the stirrups, the manner in which his legs are in contact with the horse and the position of his upper body enable him to ride so as to be "with the horse," comfortable himself and yet not making his weight become an undue burden upon his horse. This position enables a rider to place his hands well forward so as to be able to control his horse by correct use of his reins.

The fault of the greatest number of inexperienced and uninstructed riders is that they lean back and put their feet and legs too far forward. Frequently, a slump or curve outward in their backs will accompany such a posture when mounted.

The position of the upper body, excepting the arms, of the rider who is in balance is somewhat similar to that of a soldier at attention. However, the rider should bend slightly forward at the hips and it is improper for his upper body to be rigid. The frontispiece of this book illustrates the desired position of a rider mounted on a horse that is standing still. This picture of the author mounted on Reno Kit was taken at Fort Riley, Kansas, while the author was on active duty there. It is best for the rider to keep his head up, his shoulders reasonably well squared and to have his back curved slightly inward in the area starting about four inches above the base of the spine and extending about six inches above that point. It is unnecessary for the rider's chest to be unduly expanded so as to hinder normal breathing, but it is well for the chest to be thrown out slightly. This position of the upper body may seem a little unnatural at first to those who have never done any military riding and it might cause a slight strain in the lower back and at the back of the shoulders. However, the position of the upper body which assists a rider to be in balance and enables him to make the smartest appearance is worth practicing until the slight strain is overcome.

The correct position in the saddle is a most important factor in maintaining the "balanced seat." The rider who sits back on his buttocks will most likely have his legs extended forward and his stirrup straps will be on an angle toward the front of the horse instead of extending directly downward as they should. To obtain the balanced seat, contact with the saddle should be made in the manner that would naturally result if the feet were allowed to dangle out of the stirrups with the legs extended fully downward with no bend in the knees. Another way to make this contact with the saddle is to assume the incorrect position of sitting in the saddle as you would sit in a chair and then rolling forward so that the buttocks are entirely out of contact with the seat of the saddle. You will note, in assuming this position, that such contact with the saddle aids you quite a bit in maintaining the position of the upper body described hereinbefore.

The condition precedent to getting the correct position of your legs is to get a correct adjustment of your stirrups. This is accomplished by allowing your legs to hang straight down from the saddle and having an instructor or helper adjust the stirrups so that the bottom of the stirrup iron is even with your ankle bone.

An exception to this rule for adjusting stirrups is that a rider should shorten his stirrup straps by two holes if he intends to take jumps from two and one-half to four feet high and should come up another hole or two before taking jumps over four feet in height. A beginner need not be concerned about this exception to the rule until after he has made considerable progress as a rider.

Let us assume that you are an inexperienced rider and are seated in the saddle on a steady horse which is standing still, that the stirrups are the usual metal type, that your stirrups have been properly adjusted and that I am dismounted and ready to place each of your feet in the stirrup properly. On each side I would take the following steps: I would place your foot in the stirrup so that the stirrup tread or the bottom of the stirrup would run across the sole of your foot just in rear of the ball of your foot with the stirrup iron snug against the inside of your foot. It is important that your

11

contact with the bottom of the stirrup iron should not be across the ball of your foot nor across your instep but should be just to the rear of the ball of your foot.

Next, I would ask you to relax your ankles and on each side I would adjust your foot so that the toe of your boot would be pointing slightly outward, so that your ankle would be bent inward and so that your heel would be lower than the toe of your boot. Each of your feet would then be in the position in which you should want them to be while you are mounted.

There should be a slight bend in each of your knees, similar to the bend of the author's right knee as depicted in the frontispiece. You should be able to feel a light contact with the horse on which you are mounted from the inside of the calf of each leg to the area about six inches above each knee. Such contact should be maintained while riding. It is a mistake to grip hard with the knees while riding and lose contact with the horse's sides with the calves of your legs. It is also wrong to press the calves of the legs against the horse's sides while riding so that contact with the knees is lost.

There are several tests which can be used, when mounted on a horse that is standing still, to determine whether you have properly taken the balanced position which I have described. One of them is to have a friend stand alongside of you and make suggestions. Another is to look down, after you have assumed the correct posture, and see whether your stirrup leathers go straight down from your saddle. If they do, it is a good sign that you are in balance.

Another test is to assume the correct posture with your head and eyes forward. Then, while maintaining the rest of your body in the same position, drop your head and eyes just enough to look over one knee. If you can see the toe of your boot, that is a good indication that you have been in balance so that, to regain balance, all that you need to do is to straighten up your head and eyes.

ELEMENTARY   HORSEMANSHIP

Chapter III

TAKING THE REINS

It is most important that a rider should know how to take and hold the reins. This includes not only use of the rider's hands in taking and holding the reins, but also the correct position of his arms.

Let us assume again that you are sitting on a steady horse that is standing still. Let us further assume that you have the balanced position in the saddle as described in Chapter II and that I am dismounted and am going to help you take the double reins in both hands. By double reins we mean that we have a snaffle rein coming from the ring on each side of a snaffle bit and a curb rein coming from the ring on each end of the lower branch of a curb bit. If we have a pelham bit, however, the snaffle rein is attached to the ring at each side of the bit and the curb rein is attached to the ring at each side of the lower branch of the pelham bit.

Figure 1 shows a drawing of a pelham bit; Figure 2, a snaffle bit; and Figure 3, a curb bit.

FIGURE 1   FIGURE 2

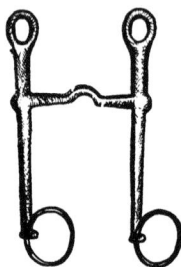

FIGURE 3

The theory of riding with double reins is to keep light contact with the snaffle bit or, if using the pelham bit, with the rings on each side of the bit. The reason for this is that if you constantly make contact with the curb rein to the curb bit or with the ring on the lower branch of the pelham bit you are going to hurt the horse's mouth and irritate the horse.

To carry out this theory, therefore, you first take the snaffle rein by allowing the rein to enter each of your hands by coming under your little finger, your hand being held with your little finger at the bottom and the thumb at the top, by allowing the snaffle rein to run across the back of each of your fingers and back out across the top of your index finger and by clamping your thumb upon the rein at the place where it crosses your index finger.

Next, I would leave each curb rein sufficiently loose so that there would be no pressure or pull by the reins on the rings by which each curb rein is attached to a side of the bit. Then, in each of your hands, I would run the curb rein between your little finger and your ring finger and bring it up until it would come out over your index finger but under the snaffle rein. You would then have the reins correctly held in your hands, subject only to getting your hands at the proper angle and to adjusting the length of the reins.

Figure 4 shows the correct method of having both a snaffle and a curb rein enter and leave the right hand.

FIGURE 4

The bight of the reins is that portion of them which is beyond the place where the rider holds the reins. This portion of the reins becomes surplus when the rider takes the reins. The bight can be thrown over to the left or the right or allowed to hang between the rider's hands on either side of the horse's neck.

The suggested angle of your hands is said to be thirty degrees off of the vertical. All that this means is that with your hands in such a position that your thumbs are at the top, you rotate your forearms slightly so that the thumbs go toward each other. Through all of this your thumbs should continue to clasp the reins where they cross over the top of your index fingers.

To adjust the length of the reins, I would first have to be sure that you were still in the position in the saddle described in the preceding chapter. If you had slumped back down in the saddle, I would ask you to resume the balanced seat. I would next check to make sure that each of your elbows would be just in front of and a little above each of your hip bones, and that your hands would be about nine inches from each other.

17

Next, and of keen importance, I would adjust the angle formed by each of your elbows by moving your forearms upward or downward and I would lengthen or shorten the distance on the reins from your hand to the snaffle ring so that the line from your elbow through your forearm and hand and extending on down the snaffle rein to the snaffle ring on the horse's bit would be a straight line, as is depicted by the author's right forearm and hand and the snaffle rein in the frontispiece.

The value of maintaining this straight line from your elbow to the snaffle ring for all equitation in which you desire to have your horse well under control cannot be overemphasized because, when you have the reins so held that you maintain that straight line, you can take the next and all-important step in maintaining good use of your hands, namely, that your contact with your horse's mouth is that light touch which you maintain with the snaffle ring by the feel of and use of your little finger. Please always remember that. You do not maintain contact with your horse's mouth with your entire hand. You clasp the reins between your thumb and forefinger, it is true; but you maintain contact with your horse's mouth by use of the light touch on the snaffle rein where that rein comes around the outside of and in back of each of your little fingers.

I would next check your curb rein on each side and, if it had become too tight, loosen it so that it would be sufficiently free to avoid any pressure on the horse's mouth. The purpose of the curb bit or the curb ring on the lower branch of the pelham bit is to exert pressure on your horse's mouth to check or to halt him. When your horse is halted or when he is going along nicely and there is no

18

necessity for checking him, you will not want to exercise such pressure and you should let that rein hang sufficiently loose on each side so that there will not be any contact with either curb ring caused by the use of your hands.

The use of the curb rein is a very important element in the "emergency brake" which we will consider in Chapter IV.

You will note in the frontispiece that light contact has been made by use of the curb rein. Such light contact, however, was for the purpose of checking Reno Kit and causing her to pose for the picture with her head held high. Normally, the curb rein should have a little more slack in it than is shown in the frontispiece.

When you are riding with only a snaffle rein you should let the rein come under your little finger and up and over your index finger, clasp the rein with your thumb and make contact with your bit by use of your little fingers. The use of your snaffle rein only is the same as is the use of that rein with the double reins.

When one is learning to ride, it is best to take the reins in both hands. As progress is made however, a rider should learn to take the reins in either the right or left hand. When on a pleasure ride or road march of any distance, it becomes monotonous to the rider to keep the reins in both hands or in either hand for a long time.

Let us assume that you have only snaffle reins and want to take them with your right hand. You would take the right snaffle rein, as described hereinbefore, by letting the rein pass under the little finger of your right hand and up and over the index finger. You would then take the rein from the left side and, by use of your left hand, run it between your little finger and ring finger and on up and through, between the rein from the right and your index finger. You would then clasp both reins by use of your thumb at the place where they would pass over your index finger. You would reverse this procedure in order to hold the reins with the left hand.

Let us next assume that you desire to hold double reins in your right hand. Again, you would start by bringing your right snaffle rein around the bottom of the little finger of your right hand and up and over your index finger. Next you would run the left snaffle rein through between the index finger and the middle finger of your right hand. Your right curb rein would then go between your little finger and your ring finger and your left curb rein would go between your ring finger and your middle finger. All four reins would then pass between your index finger and your thumb where they would be clamped by the use of your thumb.

Figure 5 depicts all reins being held in a rider's right hand.

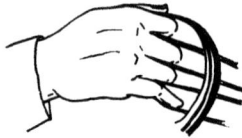

FIGURE 5

To take double reins in your left hand, it would be left snaffle rein under your little finger and up, left curb rein between little finger and ring finger and on up, right curb rein between ring finger and middle finger and on up, right snaffle rein between middle finger and index finger and on up and all reins running over the index finger and clamped to it by use of the thumb.

A study of the sketches will clarify the explanation of the holding of the reins so that with a little practice it will be easy for you to take the reins correctly. When you have taken the reins with one hand, you should rotate your forearm so that the back of your hand is out and your thumb is on top as shown in Figure 5. Each of the joints of your fingers will be bent so as to assist you to hold the reins between the places where they come between your fingers and where they go back out between your index finger and your thumb.

The biggest fault of beginners, after they have learned to take the reins with their hands, is that they allow their grip on the reins to become too far from the horse's mouth. This is otherwise known as having too long a rein. Frequently, this fault is accompanied by losing the correct balanced seat. When this happens, it is the duty of an instructor to make corrections, but if you will apply the lessons explained herein when riding and frequently check your position in the saddle and the stirrups and the manner in which you are holding the reins, you can accomplish the desired result.

Let us assume that you are holding double reins in both hands, that the reins are too long and that you desire to correct this situation. The best way is to use the thumb and forefinger of the left hand to clasp the right reins just in back of the right hand, run the right hand down until you have what appears to you to be the correct place to clasp the right reins and then do so by running your right reins between your thumb and forefinger and using your thumb as a clasp. You should then observe your right curb rein to see that it is sufficiently loose. If it is not, you should relax your right thumb and, with the use of your left thumb and forefinger, pull the right curb rein back out from between the little finger and ring finger of your right hand until your right curb rein is sufficiently loose so that it will not be the rein by which you contact your horse's mouth.

While holding your right reins at the correct place you can next throw your right reins across your horse's neck so that you can use your right thumb and forefinger to enable you to make the same type of adjustment of your left reins.

When you are using only the single rein on each side you can either use the thumb and forefinger of the opposite hand to clasp the rein while you slide your hand down on each side to the desired place for holding the rein or you can simply work your hand toward the horse's mouth on the rein and thereby take a shorter rein.

It is quite easy to get a shorter rein when holding the reins in one hand because you have a free hand with which you can hold the bight of the reins while you run the hand with which you are holding the reins on down the reins until you reach the place where you desire to hold them. Thereupon, you can use your free hand to loosen your curb reins so that neither of them will exert any pressure or pull on the curb bit in the horse's mouth.

Taking longer reins presents no problem. All that you have to do is relax your fingers and let your reins slip through them. However, if you are like most of the beginners whom I have taught, your problem will not be how to get longer reins while riding. Your problem will be how to keep the correct hold of the reins. To accomplish this, you will have to check the way in which you are holding the reins again and again.

Chapter IV

USE OF REINS, POSITION OF RIDER AND OTHER AIDS AT THE WALK, TROT, CANTER AND GALLOP

Now we shall assume that you have learned to sit in the saddle at the "balanced seat" and have been taught how to take the reins. The time would therefore have arrived for you to learn to ride at the various gaits.

At this stage of the game it would be well for me to give you a demonstration of the use of the reins, position of the rider and other aids at the various gaits, and to accompany the demonstration with an explanation of each step taken.

Therefore, I would saddle up one of my horses with a flat saddle and would use a bridle with a pelham bit and double reins. Let us assume that I would use Hercules for this demonstration. Being a half bred, he is less impetuous than the thoroughbreds, unless they have been worked for several days consecutively.

I would tell you that I was going to ride on a circle of about 75 yards in circumference and ask you to place yourself in or near the center of the circle where you could best observe me as I rode around.

Upon mounting, I would take the balanced position in the saddle and take the reins correctly, with a sufficiently short rein to call Hercules' attention to the fact that I was about to move out. This is known as "gathering a horse". I would thereupon, by the use of light leg pressure, which is a squeeze with the legs, cause him to move out at the walk. As I applied leg pressure and Hercules moved out, it would be important that my hands should be sufficiently relaxed so that I would not be exerting any backward pull with the reins on the bit in his mouth.

The principal point to bear in mind while riding at the walk is that the horse's head should bob up and down. That is the natural motion of a horse's head while the horse is walking. If the horse's head does not bob up and down, the reason is likely to be that the rider is not following the horse's mouth, in using his reins, so as to enable the horse's head to follow its natural course.

In giving you this demonstration, I would emphasize the use of my hands and ask you to watch them carefully. The motion of my hands to follow Hercules' mouth would be a gentle motion back and forth. As his head would go down, my hands would go slightly forward. As his head bobbed up, my hands would come slightly back. This is known as "maintaining contact" with the horse's mouth.

In order for my hands to carry out this forward and backward motion, I would have to increase the angles made by my elbows as my hands wou'd go forward and decrease the angle as my hands would come back.

It would, of course, be essential that I maintain the balanced seat and correct hold of the reins as Hercules walked. If he should throw his head forward, as all horses frequently do when moving out at the walk, I would have to take up whatever slack in the reins I would have lost by this motion of his head.

Here again I would emphasize the fact that my curb rein would be kept loose enough so that there would be no backward pull on the rings to which the curb rein is attached. The contact between my hands and his mouth would be by use of the snaffle rein which, as I have previously explained, is attached to the rings on each side of the bit. I would maintain this contact by the touch of each of my little fingers on each of the snaffle reins. It would be of the utmost importance that my wrists should be sufficiently relaxed so that my hands could follow Hercules' mouth without causing the bit to grind in his mouth at all so long as he continued to walk in a relaxed

FIGURE 6

manner with his head bobbing. In Figure 6 Hercules is shown while starting out at the walk. As he continues to walk out, his head and neck relax and extend farther forward.

When a rider starts out on a horse that is feeling good, which is frequently caused by the horse having had plenty of oats and no work for several days, the horse is likely to want to jig trot or take up an even faster gait. To overcome such action on the part of the horse, it is necessary to check the horse by using what is known as the "direct rein."

If I should have to check Hercules, I would clench each fist, while still keeping the reins clamped between each thumb and forefinger, and I would bring my arms slightly to the rear so that I would have a good feel of the bit in his mouth. Thereupon, I would twist each hand from the wrist in a downward and inward motion, hold that contact with the bit in his mouth for a moment, and then return my hands to their normal riding position. I would repeat this procedure as frequently as would be necessary to check Hercules and when he resumed the walk, relax my wrists so as to resume the soft contact from my little fingers to the snaffle bit in his mouth.

The procedure which I have just described with the reins is not only the means of checking the speed of a horse at the various gaits, except in those instances where the more drastic "emergency brake" which I shall describe later is required, but is also the method of using the reins to assist in bringing a horse to a slower gait and to halt a horse. *I shall hereafter refer to this procedure as using the "direct rein".*

There would be no chance of Hercules having to

be compelled to keep up the walk as long as my grip with my legs continued to be firm, but some horses are too lazy to keep walking out unless the rider squeezes them with his legs enough to keep them moving at the walk. It is rare that a kick or the use of spurs is necessary to keep a horse moving out at the walk, but when necessary either of them should do the trick, but should not be applied with such force as to cause a faster gait when the walk is the desired gait.

The desired speed at the walk is four miles per hour. Horsemen frequently call this a "four mile walk." Those of us who have served in the Horse Cavalry can pretty well judge whether a horse we are riding is going at this "rate of march". The best description that I can give you of a "four mile walk" is that the horse is moving out in a free and easy manner with his head bobbing naturally.

After you would have had an ample opportunity to observe while I demonstrated the balanced seat and correct use of the reins at the walk, I would prepare to put Hercules into a trot. There are two all important features in riding correctly at the trot. One of them is that the rider's wrists *must* be sufficiently relaxed so that the shock which a rider's body receives from the action of the horse at the trot will not cause the reins to pass that shock on to the bit in the horse's mouth. The other is that by posting a rider may avoid that bumping and shaking which he would get by riding at the trot without posting. Posting is the means by which the rider's seat leaves and returns to the saddle in rhythm with the trot.

I would put Hercules into the trot by a slight squeeze with my legs. No further aids need be used to get him into the trot. Some horses, however, must be squeezed vigorously or must be kicked or touched a little with the spurs to get them into the trot. The point here is that with a lazy horse who isn't going to do anything he doesn't have to do the rider must be determined and must show the horse that he is determined by whatever means it takes to do so and the horse will respond by going into the trot.

As Hercules would take up the trot, I would shift the position of my upper body slightly forward at the hips. At the same time I would feel for the rhythm of the posting trot. Let us assume that I would be going on the circle in a clockwise manner otherwise stated as going to the right. When riding on a circle to the right, I would post by causing my seat to touch the saddle each time Hercules' left front foot hit the ground., The rule to follow when riding on a circle is that your seat should make light contact with the saddle when the horse's front foot which is on the outside of the circle on which you are riding hits the ground. Therefore, it is also true that in posting while going to the right or clockwise your seat would be out of the saddle when the horse's right or inside front foot hit the ground. When so posting while going on a circle to the right, horsemen say that they are posting on a left diagonal.

Figures 7 and 8 are pictures which were taken with the photographer outside of the circle while I was riding Hercules on a circle to the right and posting on a left diagonal. In Figure 7, Hercules' right foot had struck the ground and I was out of the saddle while posting. In Figure 8, Hercules' left foot had struck the ground and I was back down in the saddle.

When riding counter-clockwise or on a circle to the left, the horse's left front foot would be the in-

FIGURE 7

side foot and his right front foot would be the outside foot. While demonstrating riding on a circle going to the left, therefore, my seat would touch the saddle when Hercules' right front foot hit the ground and I would be out of the saddle when his left front foot hit the ground. This would be known as posting on a right diagonal.

When I say "out of the saddle" I do not mean to imply that you should rise any great distance to post. To the contrary, what you should seek is a smooth

FIGURE 8

posting trot with your horse going at a gait of eight or nine miles per hour. To accomplish this you just simply have to get the rhythm of the trot. I recommend that beginners count (one-two, one-two, one-two) to themselves. At the count of one they should be in contact with the saddle. At the count of two their seat should be out of the saddle.

At the trot the horse's left front and right hind feet strike the ground at the same time, and next the right front and left hind hoofs strike the ground to-

30

gether. Then this procedure is repeated, again and again, so long as the horse continues to trot. As the beginner practices posting, he should also seek to avoid hitting the saddle too hard and rising out of the saddle too far. By this practice you can learn to post smoothly at the trot providing, of course, you maintain the correct position of your feet, legs and upper body and use your reins correctly.

I would ask you to note, while I rode Hercules on the circle around you, that I would continue to keep my heels down, my toes pointed slightly outward, my ankles bent slightly inward; that I would continue to maintain contact with the horse's sides with my legs upward from the calves; that my back would have a slight inclination inward above the base of the spine; that my shoulders would be well squared, chest out and head and eyes up; and that my wrists would be so relaxed and my reins so held that the shock which my body would receive from Hercules' motion at the trot would not be reflected to the bit in his mouth by any pull or unnnecessary jiggling of the reins. The rider must bear all of these things in mind to ride smoothly at the posting trot.

Having demonstrated the posting trot, I would prepare to put Hercules into the canter. This is accomplished by what we call the "gallop depart". Let us assume again that I was riding on the circle in a clockwise or right direction and that you were standing in the center of the circle watching me. I would tell you that in order to put Hercules into the canter from the trot I would slide my outside or left leg slightly back, raise my inside or right rein and drive him with a squeeze of my legs. I would also ask you to note that upon taking up the canter his right front foot would extend well forward at each stride he would take and at the same time his head would extend well forward so that it would be necessary for my hands to follow his mouth by extending forward each time his head moved forward so that I could get him to take up and could keep him in a smooth canter. Such a canter, while going on a clockwise circle, or circle to the right, is known as a canter on a right lead.

Having explained what I was about to do and while riding at the trot I would take up the "gallop depart" by sliding my left leg, which would be my outside leg, slightly to the rear, by raising my right hand slightly so as to make contact with the right side of the bit in his mouth and by giving a distinct squeeze with my legs.

This would be enough to put Hercules into the canter. When riding a lazy horse it is sometimes necessary to use a kick or to accompany the squeeze with the legs with a gig with the spurs in order to accomplish the gallop depart.

As Hercules went into the canter, I would first lean well forward at my hips and concentrate on having my hands follow his mouth by extending them forward each time his head would go forward. I would next settle down into the saddle and I would follow the motion of Hercules' head as it went forward by extending my arms so that there would be no angle formed by either of my elbows. As his head would come back at each stride, I would take up the slack in the rein by bending my elbows.

As at other gaits the contact from my hands to Hercules' mouth with the reins would be from my little fingers to the rings on the side of the snaffle bit.

My legs would be firm against his sides but would exert no more pressure than would be necessary to keep him in the canter. My seat would be well down in the saddle. My upper body would be further back than at the trot and would go slightly back, in the rhythm of the canter, each time Hercules' right front foot and head would go forward. My upper body would go slightly forward, by bending at the hips, in between each forward motion of Hercules' right front foot and head, during which time his hind legs would be coming forward.

It is utterly useless and confusing to burden a beginner with an explanation of what action each leg of a horse takes at the canter. The key to riding at a smooth canter is to follow the horse's head with the reins by taking the action I have described and by getting into the rhythm of the canter while settled well down into the saddle.

Horses will sometimes go into a "false canter" from the "gallop depart". By that we mean that when going on a circle to the right the horse's left front foot will extend beyond the right front foot. The answer to such a situation is to bring your horse back to a trot, take up a posting trot and again apply the aids described above for the "gallop depart".

In order to bring a horse from a canter back down to a trot the rider should sit well down in the saddle and use the "direct rein" which I have explained.

In describing the "gallop depart" I made reference to raising your right or inside rein slightly while going on a circle to the right. As an aid to getting a "true canter" (by which the horse's inside fore leg extends the farthest forward) instead of a "false canter" (by which the horse's outside fore leg extends the farthest forward), it is a good practice to head a horse, while going at the trot, toward a corner of ninety degrees in the enclosure in which

you are riding and, just as you are about to get to
the corner, apply the aids for the gallop depart by
dropping the outside leg to the rear, raising the inside rein and squeezing with your legs. The raising
of the inside rein not only has the effect of making
his inside shoulder more free than his outside shoulder, but also causes him to make a distinct ninety de-
gree turn in the direction toward the inside of the
circle on which you have theretofore been riding.
The combination of these aids constitutes the best
method of obtaining a "true canter".

If a horse is obstinate and persists in going into
a "false canter", you should be equally determined
to make him take up a "true canter". Unless he is
an unschooled horse, he will do so when it is clear
to him that you are going to bring him back to the
trot and put him into the "gallop depart" again and
again until you have put him into a "true canter".
The answer, insofar as the unschooled horse is concerned, is that a beginner as a rider should not attempt to learn equitation on an unschooled horse.
Such a horse should be schooled by an expert until
he will take up the "gallop depart" on the correct
lead which is the "true canter".

Let us assume again that I am riding at the
canter on a circle to the right while you are standing in the center of the circle watching me and that
I want to put Hercules from the canter into the gallop. All that this means is that I am going to increase his speed. At the gallop the speed of a horse
may increase up to approximately twenty-five miles
per hour. In order to do this, I would ride him on
a larger circle. I would cause him to increase his
speed by using leg pressure which is applied by
squeezing his sides with my legs. The action of my

reins would be the same at the gallop as at the canter except that the rhythm of extending my arms forward and backward would be speeded up in tempo as his strides were quickened at the increased speed. The only real change in my actions between riding at the canter and at the gallop would be that I would bend slightly forward at the hips as Hercules increased his speed. My upper body, however, would still move slightly backward as Hercules' right front leg extended forward and slightly forward as his hind quarters were coming forward. This rhythm would also be speeded up as Hercules' speed increased.

We would not be interested in what is known as the "breeze". This is a gallop in which the horse goes at full speed ahead. Such a gait should be reserved to jockeys rather than riders for pleasure. In such a gait the jockey bends well forward over the horse's neck and rides with a tight hold on the reins. This enables the horse to "take the bit in his mouth" and gives him the support he needs "to really run". As a beginner, this is the gait that you should especially avoid. You can avoid it by following the horse's mouth with the correct use of your reins and by proper use of the "direct rein" as I have explained it.

Having Hercules going at the gallop on a large circle and desiring to bring him back down to a canter on a smaller circle (our originally used circle of about seventy-five yards in circumference), I would shift my weight slightly to the rear and check him with the "direct rein". This would be enough to slow Hercules' speed from the gallop to a smooth canter. After I had put him into a canter on the smaller circle and desiring to bring him to the trot, I would sit down in the saddle and again check him with the "direct rein" until he started to trot. I would immediately seek to pick up the rhythm of the posting trot (this usually takes about two to four strides at the trot) and would relax my wrists so that the shock of the trot to my body would not be reflected to the bit in Hercules' mouth.

I would still be riding on a circle to the right and, at this stage of the game my desire would be to demonstrate to you the "gallop depart" while riding on a circle to the left so as to cause Hercules to take up the canter on the "left lead". I would therefore cause Hercules to turn by use of the leading and bearing rein which I shall describe a little later on and, having turned him, would take up the track on the circle to the left. By way of review, it is well to mention that upon changing direction on the circle I would now start posting by having my seat touch the saddle each time Hercules' right front foot hit the ground and rising slightly from the saddle in between each time his right front foot struck the ground.

In order to put Hercules into a "gallop depart" while riding on a circle to the left, I would place my right or outside leg slightly to the rear and then simultaneously drive him, by squeezing with my legs, and raise my left rein. I would thereupon settle down into the rhythm of the canter with my upper body and take up the "washboard motion" with my arms and hands which I have heretofore described so that I could follow the motion of his head with my hands. Figure 9 shows the author riding Hercules at the canter on a left lead and on a circle to the left. The picture was taken from the outside of the circle and was snapped the moment before Hercules' left front foot struck the ground.

Having ridden Hercules around the circle to the

FIGURE 9

left a couple of times at a smooth canter, I would bring him back down to the trot in the manner described above and take up the posting trot, using his right front foot as the key to my actions, just as I did while riding to the left at the trot before I put him into the canter.

I would then bring Hercules down from the trot to the walk by sitting down in the saddle, without posting, and at the same time checking him with the "direct rein". As he took up the walk I would again

37

follow the bobbing of his head with my hands, as described above.

There would be just one more gait that I would want to demonstrate to you, namely, the "slow trot". At this gait the horse should go at a speed of about six miles per hour. To put Hercules into the slow trot, I would give him a slight squeeze with my legs. As he took up the slow trot I would lean slightly to the rear and extend my arms well forward from my shoulders. This gait requires the greatest relaxation of one's wrists so that the bump, bump, bump, bump that shocks your body each time two of the horse's feet hit the ground will not be reflected to the bit in the horse's mouth. At this gait, though leaning backward slightly, the rider should keep his upper body erect and his head and eyes up and he should avoid the temptation to let his back curve outward. It is O. K., however, to let your shoulders become a little more rounded than at other gaits because the secret of riding properly at the slow trot is to have the weight of your upper body slightly to the rear of the normal balanced position in the saddle, thereby aiding you to take up the shock, and to have your arms extended well forward with your wrists well relaxed. Squared shoulders are inconsistent with such action of your body and arms, thereby excusing rounded shoulders at this, but only this, gait.

Having demonstrated the slow trot, I would bring Hercules back to the walk by leaning slightly further backward from the hips and again checking him with the use of the "direct rein."

The only two points that would remain to be covered in this first demonstration to you would be the use of reins to guide a horse and the use of the "voice aids."

All that a beginner needs to know about guiding a horse in the direction in which he wants him to go is the use of the leading and bearing reins. To demonstrate this, I would ride Hercules toward you at the walk and inform you that I was going to make him turn to the right before I reached you. When I would want him to turn, I would extend my right hand to the right, thereby creating a pull to the right on the bit. This would be the use of the leading rein.

At the same time that I applied the leading rein I would bring my left hand well forward over Hercules' mane and would then move my left hand to the right so that the left reins would be against his neck on the left side. This would constitute the use of the bearing rein.

I would thereupon ride off to the right, circle, ride back toward you and tell you that this time I would demonstrate the use of the leading and bearing reins to guide Hercules to the left. As I approached the place where you were standing I would extend the left reins well to the left, place my right hand well forward over Hercules' mane and move my right hand to the left so as to bring the right reins against the right side of Hercules' neck. Hercules would thereupon turn to the left. Figure 10 shows the author using his right hand to apply the bearing rein and turning Hercules to the left. Although the picture doesn't show the author's left hand, it is held out to the left so as to lead Hercules to the left as described hereinabove.

The use of either the leading rein or the bearing rein is sufficient to cause a well schooled horse to change direction. It is best, however, to use the combination of both of them. Each time after I had

FIGURE 10

caused Hercules to make the change of direction which I desired, I would bring my hands back to the normal position so that he would go straight ahead.

I would thereupon ride Hercules at the trot and the canter by use of the aids heretofore described and at each gait guide him to the right and to the left by use of a combination of the leading reins and the bearing reins to show you that the same method of placing your hands to guide a horse is used at the trot and canter as at the walk. At the trot, of course,

I would ride with relaxed wrists and at the canter I would continue the "washboard motion" with my hands even when guiding Hercules to the right or to the left.

Having brought Hercules back to the walk, I would next demonstrate the use of the "voice aids" to increase and decrease the gaits. To increase the gaits, I would use the same other aids as heretofore described, but would accompany them with a sharp command. To go from the walk to the trot, I would use the word "trot". To go from the trot to the canter, I would use the word "gal-lop", breaking off the "lop" in a sharp manner. A rider may, however, use a clucking noise in conjunction with other aids as a means of causing a horse to take up a faster gait.

To use the voice aids to assist in decreasing the gaits, one should speak to the horse in a low, quiet tone and extend the word beyond its normal pronunciation. Thus, while using the voice aid in conjunction with other aids heretofore described to bring Hercules from the canter to the trot, I would say "tro-o-o-o-t" and would say it in a low, quiet voice.

To bring Hercules from the trot to the walk with the assistance of the voice aid, I would similarly prolong the word "walk" in a low, quiet tone. A similar pronunciation of "halt," "whoa" or "ho" may be used to assist in bringing a horse to a halt.

The use of the voice aids alone is not a good practice when one is mounted. One should use the other aids heretofore described. When proficiency is attained, there is no need for voice aids. While learning to ride, however, there is nothing wrong with the use of voice aids as a means of assisting the rider to apply the other aids hereinbefore described.

Having completed my first demonstration to you,

the time would have come for you to start your mounted work. I would thereupon give Hercules a few well deserved pats on the neck and a few words of praise, dismount and turn him over to you.

Let's assume, then, that you mounted up, assumed the balanced position in the saddle, took the reins correctly and were ready to move out. For the first day's lesson I would want to concentrate on your position in the saddle and the use of your reins at the walk and would let you practice a posting trot a little.

For the next lesson or two I would again demonstrate the correct actions of the rider at the walk, posting trot and slow trot and then make corrections as you applied such lessons, just as I have described them above until you had the position and actions of the rider and use of the reins at these gaits down pat.

We would now be ready for you to start riding at the canter and gallop. The time would have come for me to give you the confidence that one has in knowing that he can prevent his horse from running away while he is in the saddle so I would ask you to watch while I applied the "emergency brake".

Let's assume that I would use my five-year-old thoroughbred mare, Zola L., for this demonstration. I would mount her, put her into the walk, then the trot and the canter. Then I would put her on a large circle of about 250 yards in circumference, increase her speed to a gallop, lean well forward and shorten my reins so that I had good control of them. While she was rolling along at a fast clip I would turn her, by use of the leading and bearing reins, so as to head her near to where you would be standing. As I would come near to you where you could see me, I would clench my left hand and put it up on her crest or mane. I would continue to clamp the reins in my left hand between my thumb and forefinger but would also use my thumb, as well as the knuckles of my other fingers, as a brace against Zola's crest. My left wrist would be fixed. By that I mean that there would be no flexibility in my left wrist. I would therefore have the left side of the bit firmly fixed in the left side of her mouth. At the moment, therefore, when I desired to apply the emergency brake I would use my right rein, on which I would have taken a little shorter than normal hold and would snap it back, release it and snap it back again. This would be enough to stop Zola so quickly that I would have to use my left arm and left hand against her crest as a brace to keep me from going forward out of the saddle.

Each time that you snap the right rein back while the left side of the bit is fixed in the horse's mouth by use of the left rein, you give the horse a good punch in the right side of the mouth. Frankly, it isn't good to demonstrate this on a well schooled horse, but we will assume that I have done so for you so as to give you confidence. You should now know how to guide a horse in a circle and apply the emergency brake so that there should be no fear of using the aids to get Hercules into the "gallop depart".

I have described the "emergency brake" as I use it. I am right handed. There is no good reason why a left handed person should not fix his right hand on a horse's crest and snap the reins by use of his left hand.

Let us assume, therefore, that during several lessons while riding Hercules on the circle you would ride part of the time at the canter until you could use the correct aids for the "gallop depart", could use the washboard motion with your hands, could follow the rhythm of the horse at the canter with your upper body, could apply your legs to Hercules' sides so as to keep him moving out at the canter as long as you wanted him to do so, could guide him to the right or to the left or keep him on a circle in the direction you desired, could bring him down from the canter to the trot and thence from the trot to the walk when you desired to do so and had at least once applied the "emergency brake".

You would, thereupon, be ready to ride at the slow trot and canter without the use of stirrups. I would, while mounted on Hercules, take my feet out of the stirrups, cross my stirrup straps over the front of my saddle, put Hercules into the walk, the slow trot and thence into the canter by use of the gallop depart. I would ask you to note that my actions were all the same at the slow trot and the canter without stirrups as they had been with them, except that my legs would be extended fully downward with my ankles relaxed and my toes pointing downward. I would thereupon bring Hercules back down to the trot and the walk, dismount and ask you to ride him at the various gaits up to and down from the canter the same as I had done. When you had ridden around the circle a couple of times at each gait without stirrups I would feel that your preliminary instruction on the circle would have been completed provided, of course, as I have emphasized before and cannot emphasize too strongly, you had learned while riding with stirrups to maintain the balanced seat at the various gaits, to follow Hercules' head with your hands at the walk and the canter, to relax your wrists at the trot, to post at the posting trot with stirrups, to avoid having your reins slip through your fingers so that the length of the reins between your hands and Hercules' mouth would become too great to enable you to control him, and to show sufficient determination in applying the aids to require Hercules to do what you wanted him to do. When you would get to the place where you could do all of these things, I would feel that you were ready to ride one of my thoroughbreds and that you were ready for your lessons in jumping for fun and to go riding at will or to ride out with other horsemen.

When I say that your "preliminary instruction" on the circle would be completed, I do not mean to imply that you would be a finished horseman or that your work to improve yourself as a horseman by riding on a circle would be completed. Again and again one should practice riding at the various gaits on a circle both with and without stirrups. It is the best means of improving oneself as a horseman.

The foregoing explanation has been given on the assumption that each of us held the reins in both hands while riding by use of a bridle with double reins. It is well to mention, therefore, that when holding the reins in either hand only, or when riding with only a snaffle rein held in both hands or only in either hand, the action of your hands and arms to follow the horse's head at the walk, canter or gallop and the use of the relaxed wrist or wrists are the same as when using double reins with both hands.

I explained galloping only in discussing my demonstration to you while riding Hercules on a right lead. A horse can speed up, of course, from a canter to a gallop while going on either a right lead or a left lead. However, in riding for pleasure, one should seek to maintain a pleasant canter with his mount well under control, in preference to riding at a gallop.

The squeeze with one's legs, which I have referred to heretofore and shall refer to hereinafter, should be applied by one's legs at the place where they contact the sides of the horse while one is riding at the "balanced seat," excepting when one slides his outside leg slightly to the rear as the condition precedent to putting a horse into a "gallop depart," as heretofore explained.

One further precaution may be of value to you. If a horse should buck while you are mounted, you should maintain a firm grip with your legs and raise your hands so as to preclude him, by use of your reins, from getting his head down between his legs. Unless a horse can get his head well down, he can not buck in a rough manner. Generally, a saddle horse that bucks is merely acting playful because he is feeling good. However, if a horse continues to buck, a beginner should take a good tight hold on the reins and then dismount in the manner described in Chapter VII.

Chapter V

JUMPING FOR PLEASURE

This book is not intended as a guide for jumpers in horse shows. I am interested only in giving an explanation of jumping which a beginner can use so that he or she may learn to jump a horse for his or her own pleasure. At the outset, therefore, I want to emphasize the fact that it will not be a pleasure to you to jump a horse over obstacles that are beyond the state of your training or beyond the state of training of any horse on which you will be riding.

I recommend that a beginner in the art of jumping should start by riding a horse over small logs, about a foot in diameter, which are lying on the ground and over small ditches which are from one to two feet wide. From such a start, progress should be made very gradually until, while mounted on a good jumping horse, you can jump an obstacle three and a half feet in height and a ditch three feet wide and enjoy doing it.

The work over logs should be started at the walk. To accomplish this you must avoid riding a horse that rushes toward jumps. Such a horse wants to charge any obstacle toward which he is headed. It is essential that a beginner should undertake jumping on a quiet horse known to be a steady jumper. In approaching a log at the walk, the rider should use the same aids heretofore described for riding at the walk and should increase his leg pressure, that is, he should squeeze the horse with his legs during the last few yards before the horse reaches the log over which

47

the rider desires to have him step. It is important during these last few yards that the rider's hands should follow the motion of the horse's head, as described in Chapter IV, for riding at the walk. In going beyond the log the horse should continue at the walk. If he should take up a faster gait, the rider should take up the aids for the faster gait for a couple of strides beyond the jump and then, by use of the "direct rein" and sitting down in the saddle, bring the horse back to the walk. Thereupon, the rider should resume the use of the reins and position for the walk.

The next step is to bring the horse up to a small log at a trot. Either the posting trot or the slow trot may be used for this practice in jumping, but we recommend the posting trot because it is more comfortable for a rider who has learned how to post at the trot. When nearing the log, emphasis must again be put on a steady squeeze with the legs while keeping the wrists relaxed. If the horse breaks into a canter or gallop beyond the jump, the rider should again follow such action by taking up the aids for the canter or gallop for a couple of strides and then bringing the horse back to the trot by use of the "direct rein" and by sitting down in the saddle.

Let us assume that you have made suitable proficiency in the use of reins, position of the rider and other aids at the various gaits and that you have ridden my horse Hercules over a few logs at the walk and the trot. I would thereupon set up a post and rail jump at one foot in height and we would start our lessons in jumping in earnest. The post and rail jump I would use would consist of two uprights with a rounded pole about three inches in diameter and about ten feet long. I would place the pole on pegs in the uprights so that it would fall off if Hercules should happen to hit it. There would, therefore, be no need for you to fear to drive him with your legs when approaching the jump. I would also place a take-off bar on the ground about six inches in front of the jump. This is not important in jumping a small jump, but it is a good practice to use a take-off bar and keep moving it further in front of the jump as the height of the jump is increased because it helps a horse to take a jump in stride rather than to get too close to the jump and then take what is called a "prop jump" in which the horse goes up and over a jump and down on the other side while covering only a short distance in the length of his jump.

Having prepared the jump, I would put Hercules over it to show you how easily he could take it and would thereupon explain to you the following mechanics of taking a horse over a jump.

A rider should select the place from which he desires to start his "approach ride" to the jump. For a one-foot jump this needs to be no farther back than five yards, but for a beginner I would recommend starting about fifteen yards from the jump. You may ride a horse on a circle at the canter and then bring him in to the place where you desire to start your approach ride or you may ride a steady horse like Hercules at the walk or trot up to the place where you desire to start your approach ride. When you arrive at the place where you desire to start the approach ride you should guide the horse with your reins directly toward the center of the jump and give him a good, hard squeeze with your legs. This should be enough to put him into the canter headed directly toward the center of the jump. If a hard squeeze with the legs is not enough to put a horse into the canter, he should be given a kick or a gig with the spurs.

As you make your approach ride you should concentrate on following the horse's head by correct use of your reins at the canter, on staying "with the horse" and on giving him a constant and increasing squeeze with your legs.

Following the horse's head with your reins is accomplished in the same manner during the approach ride as when riding at the canter or gallop. However, in the approach ride, you should lean well forward from the hips, have your hands placed well forward, have a shorter hold on the reins than is used at the ordinary canter, and have a definite but light feel of the bit in the horse's mouth with each of your little fingers by use of each of the snaffle reins.

Keeping "with the horse" is a matter of balance that only the rider on the horse engaged in the approach ride can control. You will feel out of balance if your upper body is too far back or too far forward. In either case it is up to the rider to shift his weight forward or backward so that he feels "in balance" on the horse. When one fails to bend his upper body forward at the hips he will come up to the jump with his body out of balance to the rear. Getting out of balance to the front is caused by a rider allowing his seat to get too far forward on the saddle during the approach ride or by exaggerating the bend at the hips until the rider's head is forced down beside the horse's neck on either side.

The constant and increasing pressure with your legs during the approach ride enables you to drive the horse onward toward the jump. Either the hard squeeze, kick or gig with the spurs which I described, in conjunction with heading the horse toward the center of the jump, as the means of starting the "approach ride" is used for the purpose of letting the horse know that you want him to take the jump toward which you are heading him. After the squeeze, kick or gig, the rider should relax his legs for just an instant and then start the constant and increasing squeeze during the approach ride. This action of your legs is the continuous reminder to the horse that you are determined that he must take the jump toward which you are heading him.

As you come within the last few yards of the jump it is most important that you should exert maximum continuous pressure with your legs, that you should continue to follow the motion of the horse's head by the use of your reins and that you should let the horse do the jumping.

A frequent fault of many beginners upon arriving at the jump is to relax the squeeze with their legs. This will result in having some horses run out to the side of the jump or refuse to jump.

As a horse prepares to take the jump, it is natural for him to extend his head and neck well forward and then come up with his head and neck followed soon thereafter by the spring of his fore legs from the ground. Too frequently, at the instant when the horse extends his head and neck forward, a beginner will fail to follow this motion by the use of the reins and will, as a result of such failure, give the horse a good solid smack in the mouth by the action of the reins on the bit. This will cause many horses to refuse to jump. This failure may be overcome by continuing to use the "washboard motion" with the hands, heretofore described for riding at the canter, right up to and over the jump. The extending of the head and neck is usually done as the horse is taking his last stride before starting over the jump. The use of the normal "following hand" will enable you to avoid hitting him in the mouth with the bit.

However, when a horse gets in too close to the jump, he will hesitate for a moment while placing his fore feet before starting his head, neck and forelegs over the jump. While a horse is so hesitating, it is imperative that the rider should not pull back on the reins and should continue to squeeze with his legs as hard as he can so as to avoid having the horse refuse to jump at this last moment.

When I say that you should "let the horse do the jumping", I am cautioning you against your trying to figure out when the horse is going to jump and rising out of the saddle at the moment when you think he is going to take off. The really bad spills on jumps frequently are the result of a rider lifting himself at the moment when he thinks the horse is going to leave the ground and the horse at that instant refusing to jump and coming to a complete stop. The usual result of this unhappy combination of actions on the part of the rider and horse is that the rider goes over the horse's head and lands on the jump or on the other side of the jump. The best means of avoiding the error of trying to help the horse take the jump is to pick out some object beyond the jump and in line with the direction in which you are riding to watch as you approach the center of the jump. It is well that the object should be from fifteen to twenty feet off of the ground, such as the limb of a tree or a spike or cross beam of a telegraph pole. It isn't necessary to fix your eyes

on the object during the entire approach ride, but
it is well to look at the object as the horse comes
within the last few yards before reaching the jump.
If there is no such object beyond the jump, the rider
may look off toward the horizon, or just above the
skyline. It is important that the object at which you
look or the place on which you focus your eyes during these last few yards before the horse goes over
the jump should enable you to raise your head
slightly. By doing this you won't even be looking
at the jump and instead of thinking about when
the horse is going to jump you can concentrate on
the all important factors of driving him by the constant and maximum squeeze with your legs and following the motion of his head by the use of your
reins.

While going over the jump and landing beyond
the jump you should be concerned with whether
your weight is too far forward or too far backward
and you should be careful to avoid hitting the horse
in the mouth with the bit by an unnecessary tug
on the reins. The question of whether your weight
is too far forward or too far backward is a matter
of balance which the rider must learn to feel. If
a rider's weight is too far forward, his upper body
will be well up on the horse's neck as the horse
lands on the other side of the jump and resumes
his canter away from the jump. If a rider's weight
is too far backward, the action of the horse as he
resumes the canter on the other side of the jump
will give the rider a jolt forward.

Figure 11 shows Hercules taking a jump of moderate size with the author up and in balance.

The reason why it is important to avoid having
the bit hit the sides of the horse's mouth as he is

FIGURE 11

going over the jump or landing on the other side of the jump is that such action of the bit is punishment to the horse. When he receives punishment while doing what you want him to do, his reaction may result in a refusal at a later time when you are trying to cause him to jump.

As the horse goes away from the jump, the rider should pick up the rhythm of the canter with his upper body and follow the horse's head by the correct use of the reins at the canter as explained in Chapter IV. Having resumed a smooth canter, the rider should bring the horse down to trot, then the walk and halt him when the rider so desires, all as explained in detail in Chapter IV.

Having given you this explanation of what you should do to ride a horse over a jump, I would suggest that if a horse should refuse at any time as your training in jumping progressed you should immediately give him a thorough gigging with your spurs. If a horse should run out you should immediately guide him back to the jump while remaining mounted and give him a gigging. In administering such a gigging, it is best to use one spur and then the other until the horse has had about ten solid gigs. This will impress upon him the fact that you are very much displeased with his failure to take the jump, provided you so punish him while his failure is fresh in his mind.

We would now be ready for you to ride Hercules over the jump which was set up for you. I would suggest that you ride Hercules into a place which I would point out to you which would be about fifteen yards from the jump on the side from which I would want you to approach the jump. I would also suggest that you should bring Hercules into that place so as to be able to turn him to the left and head him toward the jump and that, as you did so, you should apply the aid for the "gallop depart" so as to get him into the canter at a left lead. Such aids, you will recall, are sliding your right leg slightly to the rear, raising your left rein, and driving him into the canter by a squeeze with your legs. The chances are good that Hercules would take up a true canter on the left lead. By anticipating that he would do so, your previous practice in riding at the canter while following the motion of his head with your hands would help you to follow his head while he was on a left lead in the approach ride.

I would place myself about five yards out to one side of the jump. As you made your approach ride, I would call "legs, legs, legs, legs" again and again until you were over the jump. This would serve as a constant reminder to you to keep up that steady and increasing squeeze with your legs that would compel him to take the jump.

We would continue to work on the principles of jumping which I have stated as your lessons in jumping over the post and rail jump progressed. The secret of success in jumping is to make gradual progress until one can take jumps on a good jumping horse up to three and one-half feet, which is the size of an ordinary field obstacle. A fine jumping horse can go beyond that height and on up into the high jump class, but bear one very important thing in mind, namely, that the high jumping horse is very likely to have developed his skill by having been punished until he feared to refuse to jump. Jumping over high jumps is not a natural thing for a horse to do. When you see a horse clearing high jumps in a show, it is entirely possible that he is doing so as a result of training in which a trainer gave him sharp lashes with a whip on his rump while he was going into the jump and at the same time his rider clucked to him or used some key word such as "up", "up".

There is nothing wrong with clucking to a horse coming into a jump or using key words such as "up", "up". Either of these is a good practice. The points which I desire to emphasize are that this book is intended only as instruction in jumping for your own pleasure, that the means by which the horse you ride should be compelled to do such jumping should be the driving force of the squeeze with your legs and not punishment meted to the horse by a man on the ground with a whip, and that progress in jumping should be made by gradual increases in the height of the jumps you take.

Let us assume that as your lessons progressed and as I observed you I felt that you were not bending sufficiently far forward at the hips or that you were developing a tendency to pull back on the reins while going over the jump. To overcome either of these difficulties, I would put an ordinary belt around Hercules' neck, buckle it so that it wouldn't be too tight on him and ask you to reach for the belt with your hands as he started to jump. This would bring your upper body well forward without the necessity of you exaggerating the bend at your hips. By holding the belt while going over the jump, you would learn to overcome the bad practice of hitting Hercules in the mouth while going over the jump.

Let's assume that as your training continued Hercules ran out from a jump of two and one-half feet and that he went to the left. I would immediately ask you to bring him back to the jump and give him the thorough gigging heretofore described. Thereupon, I would ask you to dismount and let me mount. I would take him back to the place from which we would be starting the approach ride, give him a good squeeze to get him into a canter, apply the continuous and increasing squeeze with my legs and not only follow his head with my hands but also have a little heavier feel of the bit with my right hand so as to be prepared to lead him to the right with the use of the right rein if he should make a false move to the left. I would continue this feel with my right rein while driving him with my legs until I knew that he was on his way over the jump. If the run out had been to the right, I would use such heavier than normal feel with my left rein when next taking him over.

One way to avoid run-outs is to use wings on both

of the approach sides of a jump. I favor the use of wings while instructing pupils in jumping. I have described the way to cure run-outs, however, so that beginners who read this book will know what to do if a horse ever does run out while they are attempting to cause him to jump. The best way to avoid a run-out is to keep the horse you are riding headed straight toward the center of the jump while compelling him to jump by the use of your legs.

There can be no hard and fast rules as to how much progress pupils can make in jumping because some pupils just naturally progress much faster than others. One big mistake made in the days of the Horse Cavalry by some instructors was that they required riders to attempt jumps beyond the state of their training or beyond the state of training of the horse on which they were mounted. This would frequently result in a miserable experience for the rider with the result that he would not enjoy jumping until he was mounted on a horse in which he had confidence at some later time.

The best advice that I can give you, therefore, is to start on low jumps and make your progress gradually. By doing so you will have confidence every time you face a jump that you are going to make the horse take that jump. That self confidence will be transmitted to the horse by the use of your legs and reins. Conversely, he will sense any lack of confidence on your part and a refusal may be the result.

After you had made suitable proficiency in jumping that post and rail jump from which the post would fall if the horse should hit it, I would have you take Hercules over logs from two to three feet in diameter and over a row of bales of hay placed lengthwise on the ground. The same principles as explained above would enable you to drive him over such obstacles. Thereafter, you would be ready to jump obstacles combining width and height such as a triple bar jump, but I would recommend that you should not approach any jump that would be strange to your horse at a height that exceeded the height of jumps over which you had already taken him. I would also advise against your jumping a brush jump or any type of jump that a horse can jump "through" instead of "over". The reason for this recommendation is that after a horse has become accustomed to jumping "through" one or more jumps there is too great a likelihood of his hitting a solid jump. When a horse hits a solid jump the result will be that the rider will be thrown forward for several yards and will receive a rough bump on hitting the ground. The horse may even land on the rider.

If you should find yourself in the predicament of being thrown from a horse that hits a solid jump or falls upon reaching the far side of a jump your best chance of avoiding serious consequences is to continue to watch the horse and roll away from the place where his hind quarters are going to land. It may or may not be true, but experience has led me to believe that a horse that hits a jump or falls on the far side of a jump will make an effort to keep from having any part of his body hit the rider. Reno Kit fell while landing on the far side of a jump once at Fort Riley and Golden Tone hit a high, wide and solid jump while I was riding her when out there. On each occasion, I hit the ground and rolled to safety.

Early in this chapter I advised a beginner against jumping a horse that rushes toward jumps. That is good advice. However, if you have the opportunity to ride such a horse when you have ridden enough over jumps and have enough self confidence to feel that you can jump a "rusher", just start him over low jumps. Don't let friends kid you into starting to work him over jumps higher than a foot and a half. Let him jump small jumps again and again. Don't jump him more than ten times on any one day. Each time you head him toward a jump, use the principles of jumping that I have explained, but be particularly careful not to pull back on the reins or to give him a slap in the mouth with the bit by faulty use of the reins. I know that it is difficult to keep a sufficiently short rein to guide him to the center of the jump while he is going at a fast clip and also be sure not to pull on the reins or slap his mouth, but it is essential so to ride a "rusher" in order to get results from him. After he realizes that you are not going to hit him in the mouth and grind the bit in his mouth, it is likely that he will settle down and decrease his speed in the "approach ride." Much work over small obstacles and correct use of reins combined with the other principles of jumping heretofore explained constitute your only opportunity to train a "rusher" so that he may be ridden over jumps for pleasure. Through such training it is also essential that you should conduct yourself in such a calm and self-confident manner that you will exert a calming influence upon him.

It is possible that a horse that one believes to be a "rusher" is really just full of energy by having had too little work and having been too well fed for too long a time. Such a horse will settle down nicely after a few workouts over low jumps, during which the rider uses the methods heretofore outlined.

A good practice in jumping many horses, excepting "rushers" which have terrific drive forward, is to ride a horse on a wide circle beside the jump several times before putting him into the "approach ride". By such a practice you cause the horse to relax until you want to start the approach ride. Some "rushers" however, will not so relax. Such "rushers" should be given a thorough warm up before the jump is set up and given full opportunity to take plenty of low jumps during each workout.

I have referred to putting Hercules into a left lead to take a small jump. He goes best on that lead. Most horses have a preference for either a left or a right lead. On a long course of several jumps, however, many horses change leads one or more times. The rider should gain such proficiency in riding at the canter at both the left and right leads that it will be second nature with him to take up the proper use of the reins and rhythm of the canter as the horse changes leads. Also, if you start your approach ride on one lead, it is best not even to attempt to cause the horse to change leads before arriving at the jump you are approaching.

I have assumed, for the purpose of this chapter, that Hercules was warmed up by being ridden on the flat before being jumped. It is always well to ride for at least ten minutes before starting jumping in any lesson or work out. Even as you progress in jumping and are ready to take jumps up to three and one-half feet, it is also well to take a few small jumps at two feet and then bring the bar up gradually or go on to such other obstacle as you desire to clear as your objective for the day.

I do not plan in advance how many times I expect to jump a horse in a workout. Instead, I am concerned with an objective which normally is to get a real good jump at a desired height. I work up to that height from smaller jumps. When I have taken the horse over at the desired height and the jump suits me insofar as form is concerned, I make a lot over the horse by patting him or her on the neck and by use of praise. If one has a few oats in one's pocket it is also good to dismount and feed the oats from the palm of the open hand while rubbing in back of the horse's ears with the other hand.

The proper method of causing horses to jump over ditches is the same as I have explained for causing them to jump over obstacles. Here again, however, it is well to jump over small ditches to start with and thereafter to require a horse to jump over increasingly wider ones. Here again a refusal or run out should result in the rider immediately punishing the horse while holding him at the edge of the ditch and then returning to the starting point of the approach ride and compelling the horse to take the ditch by the use of the rider's legs while guiding the horse toward the ditch.

I have heard it said that when a horse lands beyond a jump a rider's seat should be well down in the saddle. This is true, but a beginner in jumping can't practice landing with his seat well down in the saddle. What he can do is to stay with his horse in the approach ride, just before the horse takes off, and while the horse is over the jump. By doing so he will be in balance as the horse lands on the far side of the jump. By being in balance the rider will be well down in the saddle.

I will emphasize just one more point. If you make a serious effort to follow the method of jumping that I have explained in this chapter and have trouble, it is likely to have been caused by a failure to keep your feet placed correctly in the stirrups. Remember, you should keep your toes pointed slightly outward, heels down, ankles bent slightly inward and the bottom of the stirrup irons across the bottom of each foot just in back of the ball of the foot. As heretofore explained, the normal length of your stirrup is such that when seated in the saddle with legs fully extended the bottom of the stirrup irons should be even with your ankle bones, but as you increase the size of the jumps you take to two and a half feet you should shorten your stirrup straps by at least two holes.

If you want to increase your own confidence and the confidence of the horse you are riding, lead him or ride him at the walk around the far side of the jump you are about to take before you start him to the place where you are going to begin your "approach ride."

Stick with this jumping. Take it gradually. Never hesitate to drop the height of a jump and start working back up when you want to do so, and you will find it the best of sport and a source of real pleasure to you.

ELEMENTARY HORSEMANSHIP

Chapter VI

RIDING AT WILL, GROUP RIDING AND GOING
DOWN SLIDES

While the explanations heretofore given in this book will be of value to riders of little experience who desire to go fox hunting, yet it should be made very clear that this book is not intended as a guide to riding in back of the hounds. Beginners should improve themselves until they can master all that has been explained in the foregoing chapters before even thinking of riding on a fox hunt.

This chapter is therefore intended, primarily, as a series of "dos" and "don'ts" for beginners who have practiced the steps heretofore explained and who desire to vary their equitation by "riding out" either by themselves or in company with others.

There are so few places left where one can ride cross-country without having to go through gates or over high fences that we shall concern ourselves in this chapter primarily with riding on bridle paths or along country roads.

It is always best that at least two riders should go together. When one rider goes out alone it is wise for him to stay in areas where he would be likely to be found if an accident should happen instead of riding through bridle paths in the woods or riding far back in the country where there would be little likelihood of his being found for a long time should he be thrown and injured.

Before a rider or group of riders starts out on a long ride a plan should be worked out so that the amount of time to be spent at the trot and at the canter will be estimated. During most of the time on a long ride the horse or horses should go along at the walk with his or their heads bobbing freely. Some horses will jig trot when leaving the stable and this decreases the pleasure of the ride considerably. Until such time as a rider desires to put such a horse into a trot, he should use the "direct rein" heretofore explained to bring a horse that is jig trotting down to the walk and thereupon relax his hands so that the horse may walk out. After this has been done enough times the horse will learn that the only way that he is going to obtain freedom from restraint will be to discontinue the jigging.

Trotting should be done in between long periods of walking. When a rider or group of riders intends to canter while out on a ride he or they should first trot, then canter and then trot again before bringing the horse or horses down to a walk. This makes for smooth equitation. Unless there is an exceptionally good reason for getting some place in a big hurry, periods of trotting and cantering should be held down to not more than ten minutes duration. I recommend trotting for the first four minutes, cantering for two minutes and trotting the last four minutes when a rider or group of riders desires to do both. In finishing a ride horses should be walked for at least the last fifteen minutes so that they may be cooled out upon return to the stable.

A road march is quite a different thing from riding out for pleasure and horses must be hardened to it before trying to cover distances. Unless a horse is so hardened he really shouldn't go more than fifteen miles in any one day. If one desires to make road marches, he should increase the distance that his horse travels on successive rides and increase the horse's oat ration up to sixteen pounds per day, on days when the horse is ridden, until the horse is built up and hardened up to carry the rider for the desired distance. I have heard cavalrymen who were experts in road marching claim that they could march a horse cavalry unit thirty-five miles a day, six days a week, and keep it up indefinitely. What they planned to do, of course, would be to start the march soon after daybreak, take a long noon halt of several hours and march again in the late afternoon and early evening. It is doubted that this would be considered fun by any civilian rider. None the less, if road marches are extended beyond ten miles, rest periods of ten minutes during each hour should be taken, at which time the equipment should be adjusted and the horses' hoofs cleaned out. If you go more than fifteen miles on a ride, it is also well to have at least two periods of five minutes each in which you dismount and lead your horse.

When two or more horsemen go riding, it is well for them to travel on the left hand side of any road in column, otherwise known as single file, with from four feet to ten yards from the croup of one horse to the head of the horse in rear of him. Kicking may result when less distance than four feet is maintained and it is an annoyance to the horse in front to have another horse so close behind him. If more than ten yards distance is maintained the horsemen become strung out along the highway too much.

It is best to let the most experienced rider or the rider on the best horse set the pace. A four-mile-an-hour walk, eight- to nine-mile-an-hour trot, and a twelve-mile canter are the best gaits when riding out.

If the pace setter takes a stream, a ditch, a jump

or other type of obstacle every subsequent rider should do the same.

The important thing to remember in taking any obstacle while riding in a group is that you should ride your own course. Giving the rider ahead of you from five to ten yards distance will help you to do this. If some rider should approach the obstacle by charging along beside you or coming in at an angle from the side, it is best to hold your horse back until he has gone on over the obstacle before starting your approach ride. The most dangerous thing that you can do when riding with a group is to come into an obstacle at the same time that another rider approaches it from a different angle. While making your approach ride you should bear in mind the principles of squeezing the horse with your legs, heading him directly toward the obstacle with your reins and following the motion of his head with your reins as explained in the chapter on Jumping for Pleasure.

When going down the road or bridle path at the trot you may take your choice as to whether you desire to post on a left diagonal or a right diagonal. When posting on the left diagonal, as heretofore explained, your seat is in the saddle when the horse's left front hoof hits the ground and your seat is raised slightly out of the saddle when his right front hoof hits the ground. When posting on the right diagonal your seat is in the saddle when the horse's right front hoof hits the ground and is raised slightly out of the saddle when his left front hoof hits the ground. When trotting for several minutes it is well to change diagonals when your back begins to feel a little stiff. Normally, it is helpful to the horse also to have his rider change diagonals at the trot.

With a well trained horse you can take up the

"gallop depart" on the lead you desire while going straight down the road. If you desire to take a left lead you would come up with your left rein, back with your right leg and squeeze him into the "gallop depart". If you desire to take up a right lead you would come up with your right rein, back with your left leg and squeeze him into the "gallop depart". If the horse should take up a false canter while you are going straight down the road it is best to follow the rhythm of the lead he has taken up with your reins and body, as described in Chapter IV hereinabove, rather than to bring him back and start off again at the canter. If you want to work on requiring a horse to take a true lead from the "gallop depart" such work should be done on the circle instead of on a straight road.

It must always be realized that horses may fall. In going across an open field a horse may approach a hole and shy off. Also, a horse may at any time for no obvious reason fall on his forelegs. If a horse shies out to the right you are likely to go off of him to the left; if he goes to the left you are likely to go off of him to the right. It is unlikely that you will suffer anything more than a slight shaking up by such an incident.

Some young thoroughbreds have a trick of whirling to the left or to the right at times. If you should ride such a horse bear in mind which way he whirls after each such incident. If you find that he makes a practice of whirling to the left you should anticipate such an incident with your right rein. The moment he starts to whirl fix your right hand by stiffening your wrist. If he whirls to the right, use your left rein in a similar manner. This will give the horse a good punch in the mouth with the bit and after a few such incidents the practice of whirling with you will be discontinued.

When a horse falls, his weight usually goes to the right or to the left. Whenever you are mounted on a horse and he falls, you should roll away from him in the direction in which his weight goes as he falls because you will have considerable momentum in that direction to help you roll away from him. However, you should use your arms and/or your legs to push yourself away from him as you start to roll. If a horse on which you are mounted should fall directly forward, you will go over his head and you should roll forward. Bear in mind, however, that horses frequently fall all the way to their knees and then regain their footing. It is usually best to stay with them rather than to try to jump off of them the moment you think they are going to fall.

I would advise against a beginner in equitation constantly and continually riding out to the exclusion of work on the circle. Riding out is fine for the purpose of varying your equitation but one should always bear in mind that he can best improve himself as a rider by practice on the circle.

When out on a ride one should work to maintain the proper position in the saddle and to use his reins properly. It is a source of disappointment to an instructor to see a pupil riding well while under close supervision on the circle and then, when riding along a road, to see him slouching in the saddle, toes down, heels up, in the same position that he could assume in a chair at home, riding at the walk or canter without following the motion of the horse's head with the reins, or misusing the reins so as to cause the bit to hit the horse in the mouth while the horse is trotting.

After a horse has gone well at the trot or both the trot and the canter and has been brought back to the walk he should be given a few pats on the neck and a few kind words. As he starts to walk out, it is well for a rider to give him a completely loose rein. The chances are good that he will walk along at the desired gait with his head bobbing freely. However, if a horse persists in jig trotting instead of walking after coming down from the faster gaits, the rider should again take the correct hold of the reins and use the "direct rein" followed by relaxed hands again and again until the horse earns the freedom of relaxed reins by discontinuing the jigging.

Some objects you may pass along a country road, such as clothes out on a line or large sheets of paper alongside the road may cause some horses to shy off slightly. The best answer to such a situation is to avoid putting the horse you are riding too close to such an object and, at the same time, compel him to keep going by applying a little more than the normal squeeze with your legs.

A truck going along the road speedily with a tarpaulin waving from it will also upset most horses. When such a truck passes, keep your horse well over to the side of the road by use of the leading and bearing reins and keep your legs active so as to keep the horse going in the direction you desire and to keep him from throwing you if he should rear up or shy off to the side.

Riding up and down hills at the walk is fine exercise for a horse. A rider should bend well forward at the hips when going up a steep hill. Horses should be held down to the walk when going up a steep hill but there is no good reason why they shouldn't trot or canter when going on a slight upgrade. Similarly, horses should not trot or canter down steep grades and riders should lean well forward when going down steep grades. A serious injury to the tendons at the back of the horse's forelegs, known as tendonitis, is likely to result from galloping a horse down a steep hill and then starting him up a hill at such fast pace.

Beginners should not attempt to take slides which go straight down for several feet before angling off at a less steep incline. To learn to take horses down slides, a beginner should start over banks or down hills which are just reasonably steep. Such practice should be done on a well schooled horse that will stay at the walk when the "direct rein" is applied. The rider should bend well forward at the hips. Placing the hands on the horse's crest will also help the beginner to maintain balance. If the horse should start to break into a faster gait, the "direct rein" should be applied to bring him back to the walk.

The objective of riding down slides is to be able to control your horse while he is on the slide and to keep him from getting out of control and coming off of the slide at a wild gallop. Leaning forward throws your weight on the horse's forelegs. He can best control his descent down the slide by the free use of his powerful hind legs. When leaning forward you are in the best position to check any attempt on the part of your horse to increase his gait. These are the reasons why horsemen, in recent years, have come to the conclusion that it is best, as a matter of balance and control, to lean forward while taking slides. It is primarily for the purpose of giving a horse full freedom of his powerful hind quarters that makes it advisable to lean well forward while going up as well as down steep grades.

Chapter VII

SADDLING, MOUNTING,
DISMOUNTING and UNSADDLING

A long, drawn-out explanation of every step in putting every different type of bridle and saddle on a horse would be more confusing than valuable to a beginner. We shall, therefore, consider the important points regarding bridling and saddling a horse, adjusting equipment and removing the saddle and bridle. We shall deal only with the use of the type of saddle that has girth straps which are buckled onto a girth, otherwise known as a cinch strap.

A horse should be tied by means of a halter rope snapped into the ring on the halter and tied by a slip knot to a post, rail or picket line before one starts to put the saddle and bridle on him.

In view of the fact that the regions of the horse will be referred to many times in this and subsequent chapters, your attention is invited to Figure 12 which depicts the various regions of the horse by numbers.

If you have never studied the regions of a horse, it would be good for you to do so. When you refer to a region of a horse by name, around horsemen, they are likely to take note of the fact that you know what you are talking about. Notice, for example, the location of the horse's "Elbow." What a mistake it would be to refer to a horse's "Knee" or "Hock" as his "Elbow."

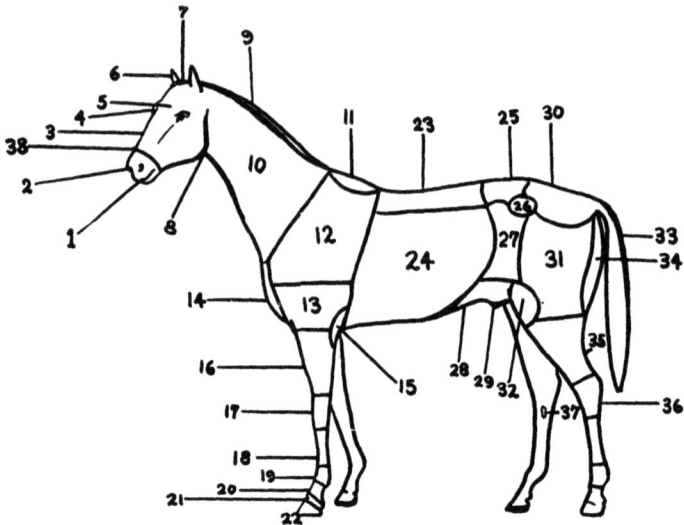

FIGURE 12

The names which match the numbers in Figure 12 are as follows:

1. Lips
2. Nostril
3. Face
4. Eye
5. Forehead
6. Ear
7. Poll
8. Throat
9. Crest
10. Neck
11. Withers
12. Shoulder
13. Arm

14. Breast
15. Elbow
16. Forearm
17. Knee
18. Cannon
19. Fetlock
20. Pastern
21. Coronet
22. Hoof
23. Back
24. Ribs
25. Loin
26. Point of Hip

27. Flank
28. Belly
29. Sheath
30. Croup
31. Thigh
32. Stifle
33. Tail
34. Buttocks
35. Gaskin
36. Hock
37. Chestnut
38. Muzzle

Let us resume our consideration of how to put a bridle on a horse.

The first step to be taken before putting on the bridle is to remove the halter from the horse's head and buckle it around his neck. This is done by un-

74

buckling the halter at the top while standing on the left side of the horse's head and neck, by using both the right hand and forearm extended over the horse's neck and the left hand to slip the halter off of the horse's head, and by bringing the buckle and strap that fits into it back up on top of the horse's crest and rebuckling it so that the halter is buckled and fastened around the horse's neck.

Next, the reins should be thrown over the horse's head and allowed to rest on his crest and neck. One should stand on the left side of a horse to slip the bit into the horse's mouth. This is accomplished by holding the crown piece, which is at the top of the bridle, with the right hand well up on the horse's head while allowing the bit to dangle just below the horse's mouth, by opening the horse's mouth from the left side with the left hand, by pulling upward with the right hand while guiding the bit into the horse's mouth with the left hand, and by pulling the crown piece up over his ears so that it is just behind the horse's ears and the brow band just in front of them.

Some bridles include a nose band. When using such a bridle it is necessary to fit the nose band around the horse's head, just below the muzzle, before slipping the bit into the horse's mouth.

One should never attempt to open a horse's mouth from the front of it while putting on the bridle because the horse might bite one's fingers. It is best to open the horse's lip with the thumb and forefinger at the left side of his mouth. If unfamiliar with the location of his teeth, look into the side of his mouth to make sure that your fingers are in the area where he does not have teeth, and then pry his mouth open with your fingers so that the bit may be brought up into his mouth in the manner we have described.

The next step is to adjust the length of the bridle so that the bit will not be too loose or too tight in the horse's mouth. When using a bridle with only one bit, such bit should be so fitted that it just barely causes a wrinkle in each corner of the horse's mouth. When using the combination snaffle bit and curb bit, the snaffle should be so fitted as barely to cause a wrinkle in each corner of the horse's mouth and the curb bit should be very slightly lower than the snaffle bit when adjusted in the horse's mouth.

Most bridles have a buckle on the cheek strap which runs up on the left side of the horse's head by which the proper adjustment of the bit in the horse's mouth may be attained. Some bridles have such buckles on each cheek strap. It is a good practice to stand in front of a horse after you have adjusted the length of the bridle so as to make such further adjustments as are necessary, such as pulling the bridle up a little on the left side of his head and pulling down a little on the right side or adjusting the brow band so that the loops by which it is attached to the bridle are just below the sides of the base of each of the horse's ears. If such adjustment causes the bit to become too loose or too tight in the horse's mouth, further adjustment of the length of the cheek straps should be made until the bit is so placed as to cause a slight wrinkle in each side of the horse's mouth. If the bit is too loose or too tight in his mouth, the horse will be irritated and this will be a very definite difficulty with which to contend while you are riding him. Whenever a horse you are riding acts fretful it is well to check the adjustment of the bit in his mouth. Frequently, this will be found to be the cause of the fretfulness. An extremely poor adjustment can even become painful to a horse.

The next step is to buckle the throat latch which is a strap that passes under the horse's throat. This should be kept sufficiently loose so that there will be no possibility of the horse being choked by it. One method of making sure that it is at least loose enough is to run all of one's fingers between the horse's throat and the throat latch.

When putting on a bridle which has a bit with a curb chain on it, the final step in adjusting the bridle is to hook the curb chain on the hook on the right side of the bit, twist the chain so that it lies flat around the back of the lower jaw of the horse, and then hook the chain on the hook on the left side so that the chain will have just a little play in it. A curb chain that is too tight will irritate a horse. A bit that includes a curb chain should include a "lip strap" that is attached to each side of the bit and passes through the link in the center of the curb chain or through an extra link attached to the center of the chain. The lip strap helps to keep the bit evenly placed in the horse's mouth. Figure 13 depicts a bridle with a pelham bit correctly adjusted on Reno Kit while her halter is fastened around her neck. Figure 13 also shows the halter shank tied to a post by a "slip knot" and snapped to the ring on the halter.

In fastening the curb chain on a bridle which has both a snaffle bit and a curb bit, the curb chain should pass under the ring beside the snaffle bit on each side of the horse's mouth. If the hook on the left side of the bit has been clamped together with the chain in it, the chain should, of course, be twisted until flat, brought under the horse's lower jaw and hooked onto the bit on the right side.

A saddle should be so placed on a horse as to be far enough to the rear of the horse's withers as to

FIGURE 13

avoid any rubbing of the pommel (front) of the saddle on the withers. In accomplishing this one should also be careful not to put the cantle (rear) of the saddle back on the horse's loin, because when riding on a saddle which is placed too far back, the rider's weight will rest on the horse's kidneys. The saddle should fit well on the horse's back with the pommel fitted at the rear of the horse's withers. Figure 14 depicts a saddle correctly adjusted on Reno Kit.

When using a saddle pad cut to fit the saddle the front of the pad should be under and even with the pommel of the saddle and the loops on the straps

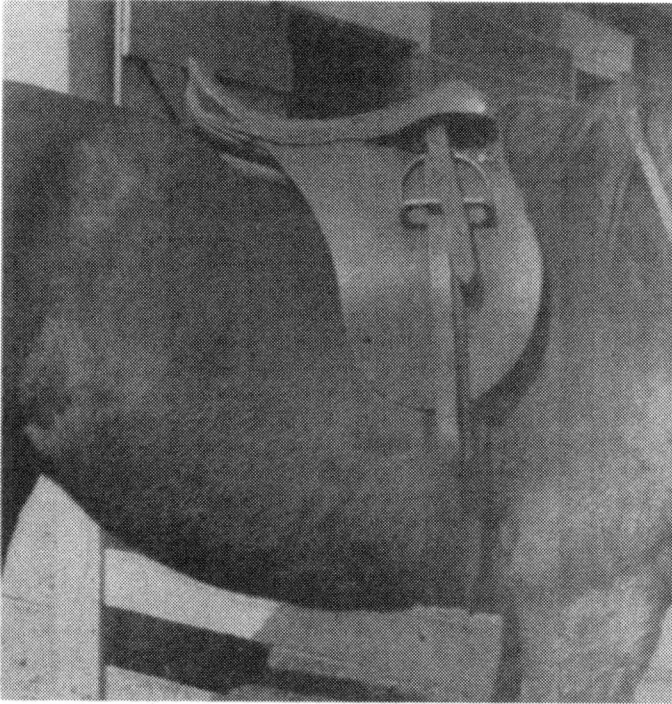

FIGURE 14

fastened on each side of the pad should be slipped over the girth strap which is the farthest forward on each side of the saddle before the girth is buckled onto the girth straps. An exception to this is made when saddling a narrow chested, large bellied horse. The middle of the three girth straps should be used on each side of the saddle to hold the strap fastened to the saddle pad because the girth should be buckled to the middle and rear girth straps for such a horse.

When using a folded blanket under a saddle, it should be placed well forward in front of the horse's withers and should then be slid back so that the front of the blanket will be 3 or 4 inches further forward than the front edge of the saddle. Either the pad or the blanket should be raised well up into the pommel arch (underneath part of the front of the saddle) so that the pad or blanket will not cause friction on the horse's withers or back. The saddle blanket should also extend several inches in rear of the saddle.

Before starting to buckle on the girth, it should be turned so that the smoothest edge is forward. The girth should first be buckled to the girth straps on the left side of the saddle. Most saddles have three girth straps and most girths have one or two buckles. In buckling the girth on the left side one should use the girth strap or the two girth straps which are farthest forward, except for a narrow chested, large bellied horse, and one should buckle the girth into the first or second hole on such strap or straps, as depicted in Figure 15. The girth should then be passed under the horse so that it lies about 3 or 4 inches in rear of the elbow of each front leg and buckled well up on the forward girth strap or straps on the right side, but not too tightly. Slack in the girth should be taken up on the left side after one has been mounted for ten or fifteen minutes.

Some horses will purposely swell up when being saddled. After such a horse has been ridden for ten or fifteen minutes, it is advisable to tighten the girth straps on both sides.

A good method of adjusting each stirrup before mounting so that it will be at least close to the correct length is to extend your left arm with the tip of your middle finger touching the top of the stirrup strap where the stirrup strap fastens onto the saddle, and then bringing the stirrup up under your left arm with your right hand. Each stirrup strap should

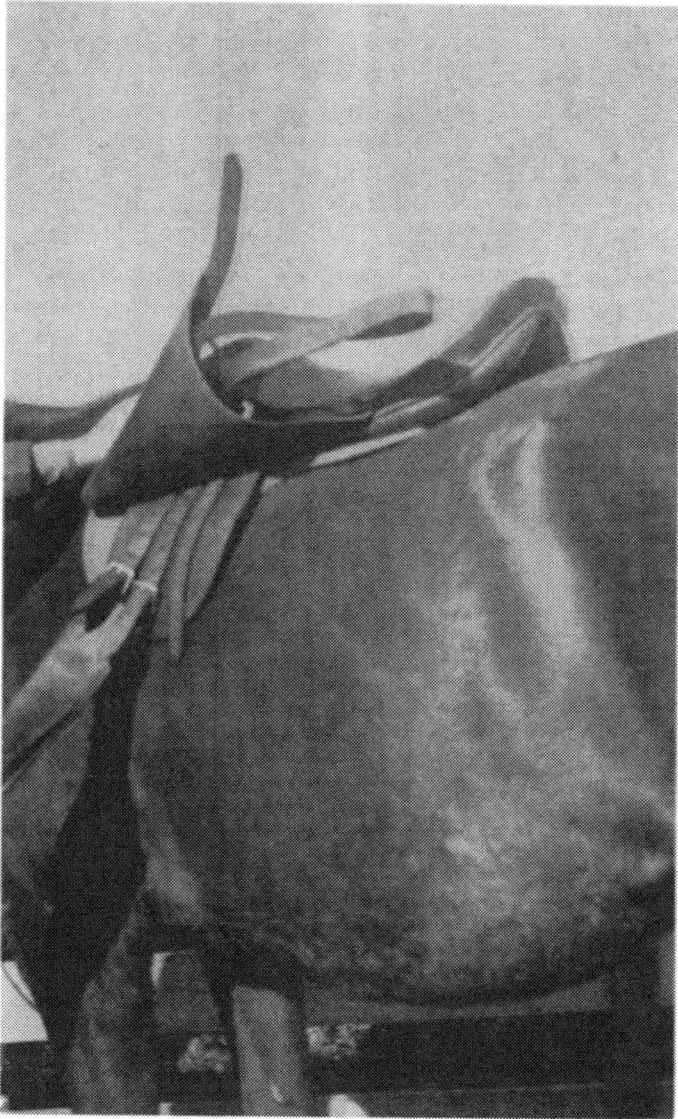

FIGURE 15

be lengthened or shortened so that the length of the stirrup strap and the stirrup iron are about two inches shorter than the length of your arm and hand with fingers fully extended.

When practicable, the buckle on each stirrup strap should be at the top of the stirrup strap to avoid contact between the buckle and the rider's leg or contact between the buckle and the horse's side. This cannot be done when using some of the old fashioned military saddles on which the buckles must be placed just above the boot type stirrup.

It is unnecessary for a rider in civilian life to feel obliged to mount or dismount in any particular manner. The first step to bear in mind about mounting from the left side is that while facing the horse's left side one should obtain a sufficiently tight hold on the reins with his left hand so that he can prevent the horse from moving out while being mounted. The reins on the left side should be separated from those from the right side by use of the index finger of the left hand. After so taking the reins, the left hand should be placed on the horse's crest. The left foot should then be assisted into the left stirrup by the right hand while the horse is being checked by use of the left hand. The secret of springing and pulling upward is to have your left knee as close as possible to the left side of the saddle. Whenever you see someone with his left foot in the stirrup struggling to mount, the reason is very likely to be that his left knee is too far away from the horse to enable him to get the necessary leverage to mount.

When you have the reins in your left hand and your left foot in the stirrup, you should clasp the cantle or rear of the saddle with your right hand. Figure 16 is a picture of the author with his left foot in the stirrup and prepared to mount. Next you should pull yourself upward with your hands and arms while springing from your right foot so that your right ankle comes up beside your left ankle as depicted in Figure 17. Next you should slip your right hand forward and clasp the pommel of the saddle. Thereupon it is easy to pass your right leg over the horse's loin and croup while the right knee is bent as shown in Figure 18, ease into the saddle while reaching with your right foot for the right stirrup and thereupon take the position in the saddle as described in Chapter II and take your reins in the manner described in Chapter III hereinbefore.

In view of the fact that most horses are accustomed to having riders mount them from the left side, it is not wise for a beginner to attempt to mount from the right side unless he knows that the horse he is about to mount will be steady. Mounting from the right side, of course, is accomplished by holding the reins with the right hand, placing the right foot in the right stirrup, clasping the saddle with the left hand and pulling oneself up while springing from the left foot.

When riders are too short to place their foot in the stirrup or are not sufficiently agile to do so, they should be assisted by others or they should use a mounting block. Any block that you can bring a horse beside which is from one foot to three feet high will serve as a good mounting block. When a rider has such trouble in mounting it is best to have an experienced assistant hold the horse from the front with a short hold on the reins until the rider is in the saddle, has both feet in the stirrups and is otherwise well adjusted so as to be ready to take the reins. It should be borne in mind, however, by those

FIGURE 16

FIGURE 17

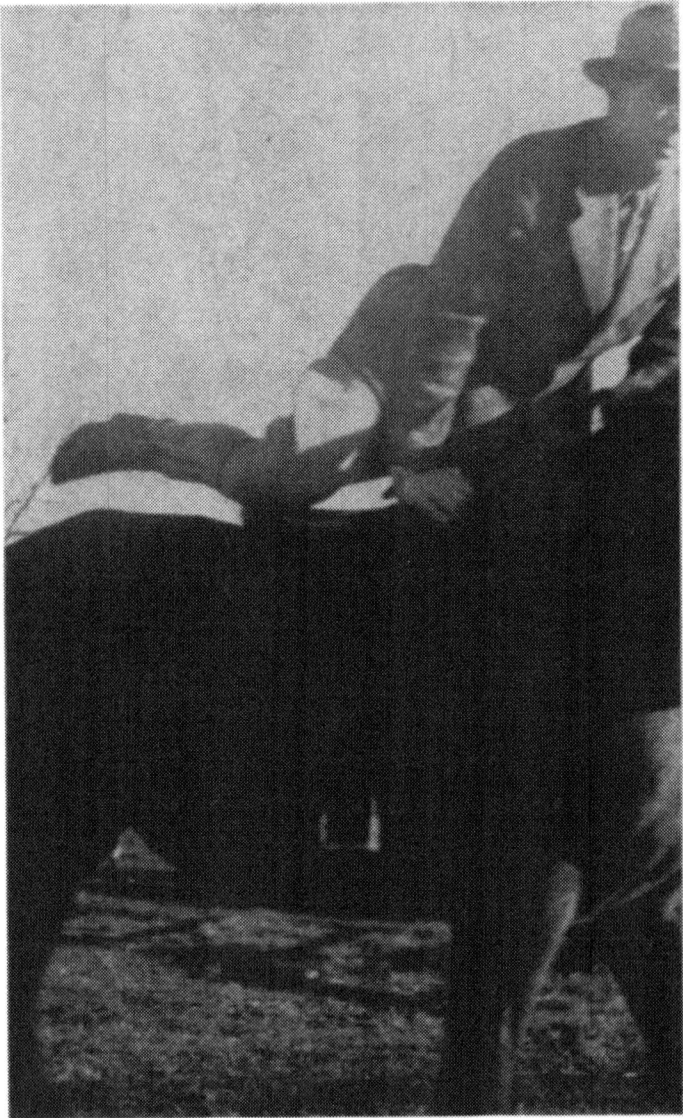

FIGURE 18

who have trouble in mounting and desire to overcome such difficulty that the secrets of success in
mounting from the left side are to get a short enough
hold on the reins so that the horse can be checked
if he attempts to move out while you are mounting,
to keep your left knee close to the skirt of the saddle, and to spring upward from your right foot and
to pull yourself up by use of your arms while your
right hand is clasped to the cantle of the saddle and
your left hand is both holding the reins and gripping
the horse's crest, without squeezing his flesh.

In dismounting, one should first take a short
rein with the left hand, place the left hand on the
horse's crest, take the right foot out of the stirrup
and place the right hand on the pommel of the saddle. He should thereupon swing his right leg with
knee bent over the horse's loin and croup, bring
his right ankle beside his left ankle, remove his
right hand from the pommel of the saddle and clasp
the cantle of the saddle with it and, while keeping
the left knee close beside the left side of the saddle
(known as the saddle skirt), step down with the
right foot. If necessary, the right hand may then be
used to release the left foot from the stirrup and
thereupon that foot is placed on the ground. If one
is sure that his horse will be steady, there is no
reason why he cannot reverse this procedure and dismount to the right if he desires to do so. I prefer
to mount and dismount on the left side and recommend that you do so, too.

One method of leading a horse after dismounting is to bring the rein or reins back over his head
while standing to the left side of his head, hold the
reins with the right hand about 6 inches from where
the reins are attached to the rings on the bit or bits,

FIGURE 19

FIGURE 20

with the index finger separating the rein or reins attached to the left side of the bit from those attached to the right side. The bight or balance of the reins should be held in the left hand. One may then move out, as depicted in Figure 19, and go in the desired direction. If necessary, one can require the horse to follow by a tug or successive tugs with the right hand. When going for only a short distance with a willing horse, one can just leave the reins on the horse's neck after dismounting and while standing to the left of the horse's head, clasp the reins with the right hand about 6 inches from the bit or bits, separating the reins running from the right side and those running from the left side of the bit or bits with the index finger of the right hand. Thereupon one may move out and lead the horse with the right hand as depicted in Figure 20.

If one is going to lead a horse for more than a very short distance, he should run the stirrup up to the top of the stirrup strap on each side if using an iron type stirrup. If using the type of stirrup which cannot be run up the stirrup strap, such as the old fashioned military stirrup boot, one should place each stirrup over the pommel of the saddle before leading a horse.

Before removing a horse's bridle one should buckle the halter around the horse's neck. To remove the bridle one should unhook the curb chain on one side, unbuckle the throat latch, pull the head stall forward until it is clear of the horse's ears and then let the head stall drop gradually downward while assisting the bit to drop out of the horse's mouth with the other hand. The head stall consists of the crown piece and the brow band.

It is best to leave the reins over the horse's neck

until the bridle has been removed from the horse's head, because otherwise one must hold the reins to keep them from getting on the ground or getting tangled up in the horse's front legs while one is removing the bridle from the horse's head. It is never a good practice to allow reins to hang down to the ground unless you have a horse that is trained to stand absolutely still while the reins are hanging to the ground from the bridle.

When the reins have been over the horse's neck while the bridle has been removed from the horse's head, the best procedure to clear the reins from the halter is to unsnap the halter rope from the ring on the halter, pass the reins over the horse's head and between the halter rope and the halter and then resnap the halter rope to the ring on the halter. After this has been done one can either place the bridle elsewhere or hold it with the crown piece fitted over one's left shoulder and the reins thrown over his left shoulder while he places the halter back on the horse's head. This is done, while standing on the left side of a horse, by unbuckling the halter where it lies on the horse's neck, holding the right side of the halter in one's right hand while one's right forearm is over the horse's neck and holding the left side of the halter with the left hand, slipping the face band of the halter down below the horse's mouth and thence up from around the horse's mouth to the area above the horse's muzzle, buckling the halter in back of the horse's ears, and then letting the halter hang on the horse's head. The face band on the well adjusted halter should be around the horse's head at the muzzle or slightly above or below the muzzle.

A good way to remove the saddle is to unbuckle the girth straps on the left, let the girth hang, go to the right side, throw the girth over the saddle and then either remove the saddle and pad or blanket from the right side or return to the left side to do so. However, if desired, there is no good reason why one should not start the procedure by unbuckling the girth straps on the right side. The girth should be completely unbuckled after the saddle has been removed from the horse.

When a saddle pad has been used, it, too, should be removed by slipping the straps attached to the pad out from the girth strap after the saddle and pad have been taken off of the horse.

It is normal to remove the halter before putting the bridle on a horse, but it is not necessary to do so. If you intend to tie up your horse while out on a ride, it is best to leave the halter on him and tie the halter rope around his neck. To make such a tie one should throw the rope over the horse's neck, make a double fold in the rope with about 18 inches of rope beyond the fold to the end of the rope, place the folded part beside that part of the rope which was not thrown over the horse's neck so that the fold is about a foot from the ring by which the halter rope is snapped onto the halter, hold the three strands of rope in one hand so that they will be about four inches long and side by side, take the remaining rope and wind it around the three strands of rope three or four times, push the end of the halter rope through the loop which was formed by folding the rope and then while holding the knot you will have made, pull on the rope just beyond the part of the rope used to make the knot. You will then have a knot securely tied but it will be one by which you can loosen or tighten the loop around the horse's neck by holding the knot and pulling toward or away from the snap by which the halter rope is clamped onto the ring in the halter. The loop around the horse's neck should be sufficiently loose so that it will not bind the horse's neck at all. Figure 21 depicts such a knot tied on a halter rope around Reno Kit's neck while she has both a halter and bridle on her head.

To untie such a knot, one should push the end of the rope back through the loop and unwind that part of the rope which was wound around the three pieces as described above. This will free the rope

FIGURE 21

so that it can be removed from the horse's neck and used to tie him up whenever you desire to do so. It is best to remove the bridle and saddle before tying a horse. If you don't want to remove the saddle, you should at least run each stirrup up to the top of the stirrup strap. If you don't want to remove the bridle, it is best to leave the reins over the horse's head and lying on his neck.

When tying a horse, the rope should be long enough between the place where it is tied and the ring by which the rope is snapped onto the halter to enable the horse to eat any hay you may put on the ground under his head for him or any grass that is on the ground under his head. When tying a horse in a single stall, the rope should be long enough to enable the horse to reach his manger or his feed box and to lie down without having his head held up in an unnatural manner. A horse should never be tied, however, by means of a rope that is long enough for him to get it in back of his front leg so that the rope will run from the place where it is tied around in back of one of the horse's front legs and on up to the ring on the halter. This is likely to result in a serious rope burn on the horse's front leg.

Another precaution is that a horse should not be tied to a barbed wire fence, the post of such a fence, or anywhere he may become entangled in barbed wire.

One of the horses ran into and became entangled in a barbed wire fence while we were out on a night march at Fort Riley. The horse became excited and started kicking and pulling, thereby getting himself all cut up and more firmly entangled. We finally released him by cutting the barbed wire, but we had a few anxious moments before it was finally over. He was a badly cut up horse when released.

Chapter VIII

CARING FOR YOUR HORSE
AND EQUIPMENT

In this chapter we will outline the rules to be followed in feeding horses and explain how to groom a horse, what to do for a horse that is overworked or "lathered up" and how to keep equipment used in riding and longeing in good condition. We shall avoid any explanation of first aid to seriously injured or sick animals for the very good reason that a condition precedent to applying correct first aid is that one should know from what injury or sickness a horse is suffering. To deal with such a subject would be getting into the field which should be reserved to veterinarians.

From a purely practical point of view, however, it is true that small cuts which do not have any dirt in them may be treated with any good medicated salve or antiseptic and will heal. I most certainly recommend that a veterinarian should be called to diagnose and treat any injury more serious than a small, clean cut and any type of sickness or disease which a horse may contract.

We will also consider one further precaution before taking up the rules of feeding. When one or more horses have just come in from a long trip by train, van or trailer, they should be isolated from other horses which are already on the farm to which the new horse or horses are brought, a veterinarian should be called to inspect the newly arrived horse or horses and to take such action as he deems appropriate, such as giving serum shots, and the newly arrived horse or horses should be kept isolated from other horses for at least three weeks. If this rule is not followed the horses already at the farm to which one or more horses have been shipped may contract what is known as "Shipping Fever" which can be fatal.

We shall not be concerned with how to become experts with a pitchfork but it is important for a horse's general good health that he should have a clean bed of straw every evening.

When a horse has trouble with one or more of his shoes, such as having one or more loose shoes, a blacksmith should be called or the horse should be taken to a blacksmith shop. Such a horse should not be ridden until a blacksmith has reset his shoes or reshod him. It is not a good practice to ride horses without shoes unless one does so only over soft ground.

It is important that all who are riding or intend to ride horses, even though they do not or may not own their own mount, should know the following principles regarding how to feed horses:

A horse should be offered water before he is given a feeding of grain. If this rule is violated and a thirsty horse is given a grain feeding, he should not have an opportunity to drink water for at least an hour thereafter because the water he would drink would wash much of the undigested grain out of the horse's stomach.

Before giving a feeding of grain to a horse that has not been grazing it is good to give him at least a small quantity of hay, preferably in the manger in his stall.

A horse's grain ration for the day (which is the total quantity of grain he will receive in a day) should be divided into at least three feedings spaced out during the course of a day. For example, if the horse's grain ration is ten pounds he should have such ration at least spaced out enough so as to get a feeding of three pounds early in the morning, three pounds at noon and four pounds in the evening. It is better to give a horse his grain ration in four or even five feedings well spaced through the day.

A horse should have at least an hour to digest a grain feeding before he is required to undergo a hard workout or before his rider starts him out on a long ride.

A horse should be given most of his hay ration for a day in the evening.

A horse should never be allowed to get to a large quantity of grain. If he does, he will be likely to eat until he becomes very sick. When given the opportunity, a horse will eat much more grain than is good for him to have at one feeding.

A horse should have salt available to him. It is good to leave a small brick of salt in a horse's feed box or to place a large cake of salt out in the pasture where he grazes.

Feed which is spoiled or dirty should not be given to a horse.

It is good to give a horse a feeding of hot bran mash once or twice a week.

A tired horse should not be given more than a light feeding of grain.

When starting to graze a horse that has not had any grazing for a long time, it is best to let him graze only about fifteen minutes on the first day that he has the opportunity to graze and gradually to increase the grazing period for each day thereafter.

The quantity of grain that should be fed to a

horse depends largely upon how much exercise he is getting and the size of the horse.

The quantity of hay that should be fed to a horse depends upon the quality of the hay, the amount of exercise the horse is getting, his size, whether or not he is grazing and, if so, the length of time he grazes and the quality of the pasture in which he grazes. A horse that is turned out in real good pasture during warm weather doesn't really require any hay, but whenever such a horse is ridden he should receive the usual and proper reward for his work, namely, first being thoroughly cooled off, next watered, then fed hay and lastly grain, and being groomed before being turned back into pasture. A horse that is living on pasture will always welcome a grain feeding. Unless a horse that has been turned out into pasture is grazing on splendid pasture, he should have at least one grain feeding of at least three pounds a day.

A horse enjoys a change in his grain diet. Although oats is the principal grain fed to horses there are many fine "combination feeds" on the market, any of which may also be fed regularly. Corn may be fed during cold weather as a substitute for oats, but preferably as only a part of a horses's grain ration. Many of the combination feeds contain molasses which horses enjoy very much.

Hay that is dusty should be sprinkled with water about an hour before it is fed to horses. If too dusty, it should not be fed to them at all.

Most horses relish carrots but should not be fed more than six average size carrots at one time. It is best to feed carrots to a horse in between the times for his grain feedings.

A good ration for a day for an average size

riding horse getting a moderate amount of exercise and not getting any grazing of value would consist of ten pounds of grain and fifteen pounds of good quality hay. When the amount of exercise is increased, both hay and grain should be increased. A horse that is a "hard keeper" will not get along well on the same ration as horses that are known as "easy keepers." Therefore, it is necessary to increase and supervise carefully the ration of the "hard keeper." Increasing the number of grain feedings each day as well as increasing the daily ration will help to keep a "hard keeper" in good flesh. When an old horse has trouble in eating all of his grain as is shown by him letting some of it fall from his mouth or by throwing some of it out of his feed box, it is likely that he needs to have his teeth filed. This is known as "floating" the horse's teeth and should be done by a veterinarian or by someone unusually well skilled in animal management.

Grooming a horse is not only the means whereby his appearance is improved, but is also important for the purpose of keeping a horse in good health. I recommend the following method of grooming a horse:

With the currycomb in the right hand and the brush in the left hand, start on the left side of the horse, at his neck, and curry and brush the left side of the horse excepting the horse's left front leg, under the horse's belly and below the hock on the left hind leg, on which areas a metal currycomb should not be used. The currycomb should be used in a circular motion and the brush should be given a powerful sweeping motion from the front toward the rear of the horse's body.

When the left side has been curried and brushed, one should trade the currycomb to the left hand and the brush to the right hand, start at the horse's neck on his right side and curry and brush his right side. Here, the currycomb would be used in the left hand with a circular motion and the brush held in the right hand should be used with a powerful sweeping motion. Figure 22 depicts the holding of a currycomb and brush while working on the right side of a horse.

FIGURE 22

There is no really good reason why we can't first curry and brush the right side. However, some right-handed people like to use the right hand for all brushing. It is definitely better to use the method hereinbefore described and switch the currycomb and brush as you change sides.

I prefer the rubber type of currycomb to a

metal one unless I am grooming a horse that has rolled in mud which has caked on him. A metal currycomb should be used with caution. One can exercise much more pressure when using a rubber currycomb.

To brush a horse's front legs and his hind legs below the hocks, it is best first to brush them horizontally, both inside, outside, on the front and in back. Thereupon, one should brush them downward. It is not a bad practice to use a rubber currycomb gently for the purpose of getting rid of any mud that may be caked on a horse's front legs, below the hocks on his hind legs or under his belly, before brushing off those areas.

A soft brush should be used to brush off a horse's head. A soft cloth moistened with water, or dampened cotton, are good to use in cleaning around a horse's eyes.

A metal mane and tail comb should be used to comb out a horse's mane and tail. One should start from the roots of the hair and comb away from them. If the comb becomes entangled it should be taken out of the mane or tail, the hair which has accumulated on the comb should be disposed of and the combing resumed. One should always avoid standing in back of a horse. To comb out a horse's tail therefore, one should stand beside the horse's hind leg on one side, comb out the tail, let go of it, walk well behind the horse, take a position beside the other leg and finish combing the horse's tail. This method is recommended because few people do a thorough job when they comb the horse's tail while standing on one side.

I clean out the bottom of the horse's hoofs in the following order: left front foot, left hind foot, right front foot and right hind foot. To pick up the horse's left front foot, one should, while standing beside the horse's left front leg, run his right hand down the horse's left front leg to the pastern and give a pull backwards and upwards. It is well to accompany the tug on the horse's pastern with a verbal command to the horse such as "put your foot up" given in such a manner that he will know that you are determined that he should do so.

While you are using your right hand to get the horse's foot up, you should have the hoof hook in your left hand. When the horse's left front hoof has been picked up, you should take hold of the pastern with your left hand while passing the hoof hook to the right hand. You are then in a position to clean out the bottom of the hoof with the right hand.

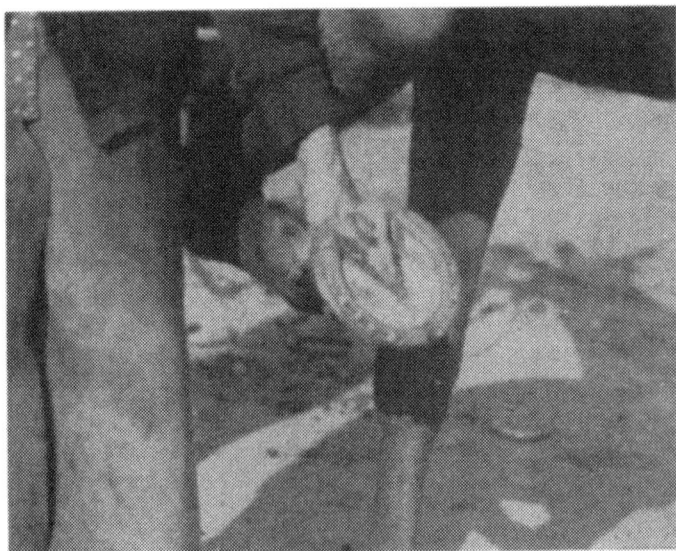

FIGURE 23

Figure 23 is a picture of the bottom of Zola L's left front hoof which was taken immediately after a shoe was nailed onto it. To clean out the bottom of a horse's hoof, one should start at one edge of the inside of the shoe and work around the inside of the shoe.

The part of the bottom of Zola L's hoof that is V-shaped and comes to a point is called the "frog." On each side of the frog on the bottom of each hoof there is a depression known as the "commissure." In the center at the top of the V there is another depression in the frog which is known as the "cleft of the frog." The "commissures" and the "cleft of the frog" should be cleaned out by use of the hoof hook in a reasonably gentle manner. Thereupon, any dirt remaining on the flat surface between the commissures and the inside of the shoe should be scraped off. The value of cleaning out the bottom of the horse's hoofs in the manner I have described is that by doing so one avoids the possibility of having a stone or other hard object lodged in mud which would cause a corn on the bottom of the horse's hoof. Each hoof should be so picked up and cleaned before and after a horse is ridden. When picking up the left rear foot, the same method is used as for picking up the left front foot.

It is awkward for me, and I guess the same would be true of most right-handed people, to clean out the horse's right front and right hind feet with my left hand. Therefore, I use the same method of picking up the horse's feet, holding the feet at the pastern and cleaning out the bottom of the hoofs on the right side that I use on the left side.

After a horse has been curried and brushed, had his mane and tail combed out and the bottom of his hoofs cleaned out, he has had a regular grooming. I like to give a horse such a grooming before I ride and again afterwards and recommend that others do likewise. It is fine for a horse to be so groomed every day.

It is a bad mistake for a rider to take such a long, hard ride as to bring a horse back to the stable in a fatigued condition. Similarly, a rider who is out for pleasure should not allow a horse to become "lathered up." The error of having a horse become fatigued may be avoided by gradually increasing the time in the saddle and the periods of time at which the horse is required to go at the trot and canter while riding out. When equitation is no more strenuous than riding for pleasure, the error of having horses become "lathered up" can be overcome by proper position in the saddle and proper use of the reins as described in Chapters II, III and IV hereinbefore, unless the horse that one is riding is just so untrained, hard-mouthed, or crazy that he works himself into a lather in spite of the rider's efforts to control him. A beginner should dismount from such a horse and refuse to ride him again until an expert has given the horse enough training to make him become a suitable riding horse.

However, let us assume that we had made the error of bringing horses back to the stable in a fatigued or "lathered up" condition. The saddles and bridles should be removed from such horses and they should be led until they showed signs of drying out. This should take five or ten minutes. Thereupon, they should have a few swallows of water. The process of alternately leading and then giving a small quantity of water should be continued until the horses were well cooled out.

Thereupon, the horses should be put in their stalls and given a feeding of from five to ten pounds of hay well shaken up in their mangers. If their stalls aren't clean and if they don't have plenty of straw on the floor, the stalls should be cleaned and fresh straw spread around for them. Also, each of them should be given a regular grooming, as described hereinbefore.

After the horses had munched on hay for about twenty minutes, each of them should be offered a bucket half full of water. When an hour had elapsed from the time when they were first put in their stalls, each of them should be offered all of the water they would want to drink and thereupon each of them should have a light grain feeding of two to three pounds. Thereafter, they should be allowed to rest until their regular feeding schedule was resumed or, if the day should be clear and warm, there would be no harm in putting them out into pasture.

The steps of watering, feeding a small quantity of hay, grooming and giving a grain feeding can be taken care of much more expeditiously in caring for a horse that has not been overworked or "lathered up" and comes back to the stable in good condition and well cooled off. The steps of caring for a horse under these circumstances may be started by offering him all of the water that he wants to drink.

When a saddle has been taken off a horse, it is good to unbuckle the girth from the saddle and, if the saddle pad is attached to the saddle, to remove it. Neither the saddle, the pad or blanket, the girth or the bridle should be placed in the dirt. However, if the sun is shining and one can hang the bridle in the sunshine and lay the other equipment out on the grass to dry out, it is a good practice to do so.

All leather on saddles, bridles, girths and cavessons should be cleaned regularly with saddle soap. Use of saddle soap on leather also has a preserving effect and keeps leather from becoming hard and dry. Saddle soap may be rubbed onto leather by use of a sponge, a soft dry cloth, or a cloth that has been dampened and well wrung out.

When a piece of leather is hard, it can best be loosened up by rubbing Neat's-foot Oil on it. Generally, it is best in applying it to put the Neat's-foot Oil on a cloth and rub the oiled part of the cloth over the surface of the leather which you desire to soften up. It is not a good practice to use Neat's-foot Oil on the seat or skirts of a saddle unless you also rub the saddle well with a clean cloth several times before you use it again. Otherwise, the Neat's-foot Oil from the saddle will be likely to make a stain on your breeches. Neat's-foot Oil and saddle soap are available at most saddlery shops and shoe repair shops.

Bits should be clean before being put into a horse's mouth. After bits have been used, they should be wiped with a clean damp cloth and then dried with a clean dry cloth. It is a good practice to clean the curb chain at the same time that you clean the bit or bits.

In closing this chapter, I want to emphasize the fact that the rider who enjoys caring for his horse as well as riding him will, by so caring for his horse, go a long way toward establishing that team work which makes for pleasant and enjoyable riding.

Chapter IX

LONGEING

Longeing is the means whereby a horse may be exercised without being ridden. In the training of remounts there are other reasons for longeing them, but the beginner should not be concerned with the training of horses so we shall not take up the matter of longeing an unschooled horse.

The first step in preparing to longe a horse is to fasten a cavesson on his head. A cavesson is a piece of leather equipment which has a heavy "noseband" which is padded with felt on the inside or part that fits around the horse's head just above his muzzle and just below his cheek bones. This noseband has a buckle on one side and strap on the other so that it may be buckled underneath the horse's head. On the front of this noseband a metal ring is attached. From each side of this noseband a strap known as the "cheekstrap" goes up each side of the horse's head to the "crown piece" which runs in back of the horse's ears.

The cavesson also has a strap which goes across the horse's forehead in front of his ears which is known as the "brow band", a strap known as the "throat latch" that comes under the horse's throat and is buckled on each side of the horse's throat, and a strap known as the "jowl strap" that comes under the horse's lower jaw and is buckled on the left side.

In fastening the cavesson on the horse's head one should first place the "crown piece" in back of and the "brow band" in front of the horse's ears.

The "throat latch" should be buckled sufficiently loosely so that it will not bind the horse's throat while he is being longed. The "jowl strap" should be buckled securely and the "noseband" should be buckled tightly.

The next steps in preparing to longe a horse are to put on gloves and to secure the longe to the ring on the noseband of the cavesson and fold the longe in one of your hands. A longe is a strap of webbing about thirty feet long. It has a metal snap fastener on one end which is used to secure the longe to the ring on the noseband. The other end of a longe has a loop in it. In folding the longe, one should hold the end of the loop in one hand and with the other hand drop about one and a half feet of the longe to the left and about one and a half feet to the right, thereby making a figure of eight held in the hand in which you want to fold the longe. One should continue to make these figures of eight until he has taken up all of the slack and is holding the longe with only about a yard of longe line from his hand to the ring on the noseband of the cavesson.

The only other piece of equipment needed in longeing is a long longeing whip.

Let's assume, therefore, that I am about to demonstrate longeing by using my mare Reno Kit. She is well trained in longeing. Having put the cavesson on Kit's head and fastened the buckles as previously explained, I would put on my gloves and secure the metal snap on the end of the longe to the ring on the noseband of the cavesson. If intending to longe her to the left, I would take the loop in the end of the longe in my left hand and fold the longe in figures of eight until there was only about one yard unfolded from my hand to the ring on the noseband.

Should Kit move out at all while I was preparing to longe her, I would halt her by use of the word "whoa" spoken in a soft and prolonged manner. I would then stretch the one yard of longe line from my hand to the buckle so that it would be comparatively tight. I would thereupon take the whip in my right hand and would face her left haunch. Having made these preparations as depicted in Figure 24, I would be ready to start her longeing at the

FIGURE 24

walk. To do this I would give the command "walk" spoken in a sharp manner. With Kit going at the walk and desiring to get her to trot, I would give her the command "trot" in a sharp manner with a rising inflection of my voice. After she had trotted a while and when desiring to cause her to canter, I would give her the command "gallop" with a rising inflection on the last syllable of that word. All the while that Kit was being longed I would continue to turn around as much as was necessary so that I would constantly keep facing her left haunch except that, when giving commands, I would turn my head to look at her head. This would mean that as she went forward on a circle around where I was standing I would have the means of compelling her to keep moving by use of the whip held in my right hand should same become necessary. As she increased her speed I would give her more longe line so that the circles she would circumscribe would become increasingly larger. After she took up the canter, I would let the longe line all of the way out so that I would have a hold on the loop with my left hand with the line completely extended so that Kit would be going on a circle of about sixty feet in diameter. The longe line is almost completely let out in Figure 25, which shows Kit going at an easy canter on a circle to the left. It is difficult, of course, for a horse to gallop on too small a circle.

If Kit should decrease her gait without being commanded to do so, I would immediately flick the whip with my right hand while commanding the faster gait by use of the appropriate word, namely, "trot" or "gallop". In bringing Kit from the gallop or canter to the trot, I would use the word "tro-o-o-t" in a quiet, soothing tone and would prolong the pronunciation of the word.

When horses are full of pep they want to run and it is sometimes a little difficult to bring them from the gallop or canter to the trot by use of your voice alone. This is when the longe attached to the cavesson firmly clamped on the horse's head gives one who is longeing a horse a terrific advantage as

FIGURE 25

far as leverage is concerned. When a horse refuses to obey the voice commands to reduce speed from the gallop or canter, one should place the whip under his arm and use the whip hand to fold the longe, in figures of eight again, over the hand in which the longe is held until he has a tight hold on the line from his hand to the ring on the noseband and has the horse going on a small circle. Thereupon, by jerking on the longe as you use the word to decrease the gait in a soothing, quiet and prolonged manner, you can get the horse to reduce his speed. Normally, this procedure is not necessary with Kit, but it is necessary when she has had little exercise for some while prior to being longed.

The same procedure is used to bring a horse from the trot to the walk except that the word "walk" is spoken in the same quiet, prolonged way. After the horse has walked a while and in order to bring the horse to a halt, one of the words "ho," "whoa" or "halt" should be used in the same tone of voice and prolonged manner. If necessary, the voice commands should be accompanied by tightening and giving jerks on the longe line.

In order to longe Kit on a circle to the right after I had finished on the circle to the left, I would give her a few pats on the neck and a few words of praise, transfer the longe to my right hand and the whip to my left hand, step around in front of her, halt her by use of a tight longe line from my right hand to the ring on the noseband and the word "whoa" until I was ready for her to start. Then, by use of the same commands and methods which I

FIGURE 26

FIGURE 27

have described, I would require her to longe on a circle to the right. Figure 26 shows Kit going at the walk and Figure 27 shows her going at the canter while being longed on a circle to the right.

After a horse has been longed for several minutes, the control which one obtains is generally much better than when longeing is first started. For purposes of assuring oneself that the horse is well under control, it is good to let out the longe line, while the horse is at the walk, until one has the horse walking on the circle with the line completely extended. Thereupon, one should command the horse to halt, as described above, and when the horse halts should immediately start to compliment the horse and walk toward the horse while taking up the figures of eight in the longe line. It is always good when a horse has been longed on a circle to the right or to the left and before changing over, as well as when finishing longeing, to give the horse a few pats on the neck and a few kind words, if the horse has done well.

Much can be accomplished by jumping a horse on a longe. One should set up the jump and then start to longe the horse on a circle so that the horse will pass beside the jump. When the horse is going along beside the jump at a smooth canter and starting the circle by which one intends to drive the horse into the jump, it is well to use the words "this time". Repeatedly doing this enables the horse to know that he should take up the speed that he desires for his approach to the jump. When the horse is on the way around the circle the handler must control the longe line so as to bring the horse into the jump. During the last few strides before the horse arrives at the jump one should have the whip handy and should have placed himself so as to be a little behind the horse and running in a line parallel to the horse's course so that one may use the whip if there is any indication of the horse refusing to jump and so that one may speed up as the horse goes over the jump and slow the horse down by use of his voice, or turn him back out from the other side of the jump without having the horse take up all of the slack in the line and get a jolt when the line is all out and the person longeing him is holding the loop on the end of the longe line. Figure 28 shows the author longeing Reno Kit over a jump.

It is best to have a wing, wall, fence or railing alongside the jump on the other side from where you longe the horse before bringing him into the

FIGURE 28

jump. It is also best to have a long, curved pipe attached to the post on the side of the jump where you longe the horse before bringing him into the jump. Such a pipe, as shown in Figure 28, should go out from the jump toward the approach side for several yards and curve toward the ground. At the end of the curve it should either be placed on the ground or it should be fixed into the ground by means of a spike. As a horse is driven into the jump, the wing, wall, fence or railing on the far side and the pipe on the near side assist one in avoiding a run-out. The longe line runs smoothly over the pipe and on off beyond the jump.

Without such facilities, it takes real skill to lift the longe just as the horse starts to jump so as to avoid having the longe line become tangled around the post on the near side of the jump. However, the use of brush piled up, or a long thin pole running up to the top of the post on the far side and the use of a long thin pole attached to the top of the post on the near side constitute reasonable substitutes which can be used on the approach side of jumps. I would recommend, however, that one should not use such substitutes unless he is going to longe a very well schooled horse over a jump. If there is any doubt, it would be best not to try to longe a horse over a jump until the best facilities are available.

As in jumping when mounted, the size of the jump should be increased gradually when requiring a horse to go over it on the longe.

Many experts whom I have known, while longeing a horse on a circle to the left, will hold the whip and the figures of eight on the end of the longe line in the right hand and take up or let out the longe line by use of the left hand. When longeing on a circle to the right the use of their hands is reversed. This method may have some advantage in maintaining continuous contact with the use of the longe line. However, I have become accustomed to the method described earlier in this chapter and prefer it because it enables the handler to have greater freedom in using the whip.

Longeing is a splendid means of exercising a horse that has a sore back or any type of saddle sore. From twenty minutes to a half an hour of longeing, either all on the flat or mostly on the flat and requiring the horse to jump several times, gives a horse enough exercise for one day. It is a good practice, when giving a horse a workout on a longe, to alternate the direction of the circle on which you longe the horse every four or five minutes.

Chapter X

SUMMATION

The foregoing chapters have been written with the purpose in mind of explaining to an inexperienced rider the things that he should or should not do in learning to ride a well trained, steady riding horse. No effort has been made to take up the problems of horsemen who attempt to break and train green horses, otherwise known as Remounts, or who attempt to cure horses with defects such as throwing their head, carrying their head too high or just plain wildness or craziness. The point cannot be emphasized too strongly that inexperienced riders should not attempt to learn to ride horseback on any type of a horse other than a well trained, steady riding horse.

It would be impossible for anyone to lay down a set of rules and say that if one follows those rules he will never be injured while riding horseback or when working around horses. To the contrary, I have known of fine horsemen suffering serious injuries as a result of jumping horses. Even when riding on level ground a horse may fall or shy off so as to cause his rider to become unseated. One who rides horseback is going to have a fall once in a while and he should expect such an occurence and not be surprised when it happens.

On the other hand, if you carefully study the method of riding explained in Chapters II, III and IV; if you apply such lessons to improving yourself as a horseman while riding only well trained and steady horses; if you make gradual progress in jumping as described in Chapter V and do not attempt to take jumps beyond your state of training or your horse's state of training or ability; if, when riding out in company with others, you do not ride your horse too closely behind a horse in front of you, await your turn to jump any obstacle and make sure that you have a clear approach to the obstacle before you start your horse toward it; if, when you are around horses tied on a post, picket line or in a stall, you first let them know that you are there and never walk or stand just back of a horse's hind legs; and if in applying the methods explained in the foregoing chapters you develop the ability to let the horse know that you are the master of his conduct and maintain that self-confidence when mounted or around horses, it is unlikely that you will ever receive any more than just minor shake-ups or bruises. On the other side of the ledger you should derive real satisfaction and pleasure from the progress you will make as a horseman, the splendid appearance that one makes when riding by using the "balanced seat" and the fact that you will become able to take a good ride without causing the horse to become all "lathered up" and exhausted.

Again, I caution you against slumping back in the saddle and letting your grip on the reins slip until the distance becomes too great between your hands and the rings by which the reins are attached to the bit or bits. One pupil whom I have taught who has read this script has suggested that I mention that in taking the proper position in the balanced seat for the first time a beginner feels that he is slightly overbalanced to the front. If so, this feeling is not an excuse for slumping back in the saddle and thereby getting completely out of balance. It is most assuredly worth while to seek the proper balanced position in the saddle again and again when riding until such position becomes the natural one for you to assume.

When you have done all other things well you may still have one difficulty, namely, allowing your elbows to wave in the air like wings while riding at the canter. This difficulty can be overcome by concentrating on following the horse's head with your hands while bending your elbows and keeping them in the same position instead of waving them.

It is the author's sincere desire that this book shall be of great value to those inexperienced riders who desire to improve themselves as horsemen. We have confidence that by study and application of the explanations made hereinabove an inexperienced rider will derive greater pleasure from riding, will present a smarter appearance when mounted and will make such progress in riding that it can be said of him that he and the horse he rides constitute a team.

FINIS

CPSIA information can be obtained
at www.ICGtesting.com
Printed in the USA
BVHW032048250822
645400BV00009B/769

9 781494 012489